TENDER MISCARRIAGE
AN EPIPHANY

TENDER MISCARRIAGE
AN EPIPHANY

Paula Saffire

HARBINGER HOUSE
Tucson

Most of the names and places in this book have been changed to preserve anonymity. Well-known guides have been given their real names. The story is, to the best of my knowledge, true.

Harbinger House, Inc.
Tucson, Arizona
© 1989 by Paula Saffire
All Rights Reserved
Manufactured in the United States of America
This book was set in 11 on 14 Aldus
Design by Nancy Brennan

Library of Congress Cataloging in Publication Data
Saffire, Paula, 1943–
    Tender miscarriage : an epiphany / by Paula Saffire.
        p.   cm.
    ISBN 0-943173-38-8 : $9.95
    1. Saffire, Paula, 1943–
—Health.   2. Miscarriage—Patients—United States—
Biography.   I. Title.
RG648.S23   1989   618.3'92'0924—dc19   [B] 89–1835

For the one I call
the Golden Lady,

and for all those who said
or would have said, "How sad."

Thanks to

My husband, daughter, and son, who lived through it with me. We share more than can be said.

Baba, who transformed my life and taught me of darshan, meditation, and mantra.

The principal and three special teachers whose clear, kind, and energetic presence supported me at school and whose sympathy called forth this book.

Caroline Myss and Pat Rodegast, for giving their time and talent.

Robert Monroe, at whose institute the "word was made flesh" and my intention to write this book was firmed.

Carole, my roommate at the institute, who crystallized my confidence in communication with her gift and explanation.

Michael and Rebecca, for a job which left me time to write, in a school which does not diminish the life-force of children.

My mother, Rose, and Zdenek, vital links between the manuscript and the published book.

My husband, again, for careful reading and for penetrating suggestions which forced me to see where I was not yet clear.

Barbara, for criticisms given with skill, gentleness, and generosity of spirit.

Jean, teacher, friend, and presiding angel of the manuscript, who always seems to appear at crucial moments of my life.

All great writers whose words have made my world more beautiful, among them Sappho, Heraclitus, and Plato; William Blake, Shakespeare, and Rilke.

The many modern authors whose words or ideas have influenced my own, among them Charles Hogue, Madeleine L'Engle, Edwin Abbot, Robert Monroe, and Joseph Chilton Pearce.

The host of helping spirits, not all of whom I know: the Golden Lady, of course, and Genesis, Emmanuel, the Comforter, the Explainer, and whatever other beneficent beings stand at my elbow as I type.

TENDER MISCARRIAGE
AN EPIPHANY

Part One

I remember your first signature well. Then, of course, I did not know it was you. It was only later—so much later, after the birth and death, after the visit was over—that I began to piece together the bits of evidence, the puzzles, the impossibilities; and then I could realize that there had been a visit after all.

It was a surge of power, and a vision, your first signature: something utterly discontinuous from what came before and which altered all that followed. Seconds before I had been making love with Michael, and seconds after I was again. There was only this brief but unmistakable interlude, this unforgettable surge of power:

I am a cliff's edge. And I am the ocean. The sky is gray; there is dense mist everywhere. I hear the crash of my waves, and I find my own sound thrilling. I look down at my feet at the foot of the cliff. Amidst all this splash and roar, I see eddies where the receding waters of my tide are held in the hollows of an enormous rock formation. In one of the eddies, in the frothy grey green water, I recognize the pieces of my enemy. He seems small. His clothes are brightly colored, like a costume. He is a broken doll. Nothing to me. I feel no sense of threat and no sense of triumph. I watch the broken pieces as they are pulled and turned by my currents, unable to leave their rock receptacle. They are lifeless, powerless, moved only by the swirling forces of my waters.

The man in my vision had been the source of pain for months. He was the principal of the school in western Massachusetts where I had been a teaching intern. I tried to believe that my fear of him was something ordinary, based on the power of his position. But I knew that there was more to it than that. He had an uncanny ability to drain the life-force of others, to sap their energy by some secret assault.

It was late spring, and I had only the summer to find a teaching job, or else be faced with another empty year at home. I dreaded the blank on job application forms that called for the principal's name since I knew this man would gladly give me a poor recommendation to satisfy his lust for harm. Filling out those forms, I had to force my fingers to write each letter of his name. And as I did, I would feel my hopes shrivel like marigolds after a frost.

In my vision I was the ocean, too powerful to have felt any fear. And later—when I had returned to my smaller self— as the tongue seeks out a sore spot to feel the pain again, my mind went searching for its old, familiar fear and found that it was gone. Although the principal remained the focus of some practical concerns, I never feared real harm from him again.

At the time this seemed to exhaust the significance of the vision, to reveal its full import. Only later would I recognize that there was more and know it as the annunciation of your visit. That lovemaking was our introduction, and that vision the first of your many gifts to me.

Shall I go on to tell the tale? You know it as well as I, my dear, having lived it from the inside. And yet I am drawn to the telling. Perhaps this is my way of trying to prolong your visit. Or do I sense that you are gone, and is this how I try to call you to me once again?

After that first signature I knew nothing of you for months. And then your presence was evident. But again, I could not recognize it. I thought that I had changed, that my heart had grown bigger. I did not realize that the love was you in me. I did not realize that until afterwards, when you had come and gone and my heart was human-sized again.

Looking back, I can see why you might have visited, although the grace of it will never stop surprising me. I needed you. I had been through years of suffering: of drying up, of boredom, of hesitation, and now, most recently, of the anxieties of an attempt to move out and change my situation. To this catalog of despair I was about to add the torment of an exhausting job. And you, with your deft timing, foresaw it all. You foresaw the need and did the preliminaries, prepared yourself a form so that you could visit me when I most needed it. I am grateful.

I had spent many happy years at home as a full-time wife and mother, and later as a meditator, too. I felt my spirit ascending in those early years. I was in a hot-air balloon, floating lightly above the surface of ordinary life, each year reaching new heights—new experiences in meditation, new insights—and even dipping down occasionally to learn new life skills. And then it all stopped.

One after another, the activities which gave me joy dried up. First meditating went, then chanting, and then even the contemplation of my beloved philosophy, Kashmir Shaivism. This was on the spiritual side. But other joys went too. Happy times with my family became more and more sporadic. And familiar occupations, such as baking bread or walking in the woods with my dog, ceased to bring me comfort. My life came slowly to a standstill.

For three years I stayed in this stuck elevator car, waiting for it to move. At first I did not even try to leave, for I remembered how high the elevator had taken me—such ecstasy and insights, such periods of exaltation in those early years—and I clung to the belief that this was a test, and things would change. "If I am patient enough," I thought, "if I am surrendered enough, I will be shown the next step." But I never was.

Since meditation was not working, I adopted as a spiritual practice to be utterly attuned to my impulses, believing that guidance would come to me through them. I tried to put my ear to the ground of my own personality. I learned to hear even the whisper of an impulse, almost before it arose. After three years of this I was profoundly depressed, lucky if I had an impulse at all. Truly, if I wanted butter on my toast, it seemed a miracle.

I can remember a friend telling me he was trying to rid himself of anger. "Anger!" I was thinking. "You're so lucky, and you don't know it. You mean you actually have a feeling rise up in you? And you want to squelch it? My goodness, if I could feel an honest flash of anger now, I'd jump for joy." And a more poignant realization came when I was talking with another friend at the dining room table. Noticing his eyes light up, I followed his gaze to see why: There was a cardinal at the bird feeder out the window. "Ah," I sighed inwardly, "my eyes used to light up when I saw a cardinal." At that moment I realized I had lost everything.

Then began my move out. It came at first as a vague stirring, an urge, which arose once in a while, to get a job. At first I did not respect the urge. I had been accustomed to living my life with an eye on eternity. If I was content staying home to cook, clean, and watch my children grow, it was because I saw all this as fulfilling a centuries-old pattern of existence, one that seemed to me to offer great satisfaction and, once I started to meditate, great spiritual opportunity as well.

When the urge to get a job came along, I felt that I had fallen prey to what I saw as a twentieth century malaise— the woman's feeling of not being useful, not being interesting and, worst of all, not being valued unless she had an outside job. But the pressure of my mounting depression overcame all my resistance. I began to suspect that the elevator was permanently stuck, and I could stay in it no longer. I started to make plans.

My plans always centered around children and school. I considered working as a school bus driver, then as a school secretary, and finally as a schoolteacher. I see now that the job was of lesser importance. What mattered was the move out. I was learning my own power. I was learning that I was the creator of my life and that nothing, except depression, was going to happen unless I created it. Nothing.

I already had a Ph.D. from Harvard in the classics. I had taught college classes in ancient Greek, and tutored Sanskrit as well. But now I went back to school to retrain. I enrolled at the local university, did my student teaching, and after two years had an elementary schoolteacher's certificate. The summer of 1985 found me, at the age of forty-two, looking desperately for a job.

I can remember driving through small towns on the way to a family vacation in Cape Cod, eyeing every elementary school with hunger—just like a man, I mused, looking with lust at every woman he passes. I was prepared for anything—distant commutes or even living away from home weekdays—in order to take a school job somewhere. A job, I thought, would keep away depression. It seemed to me that I must teach next year or die.

Jobs were scarce. There were few openings in my area, some with over one hundred applicants. I did the usual—sent résumés, was interviewed occasionally, and mostly was not interviewed because of that familiar handicap, "lack of experience." At one point Michael returned from a workshop and spoke of a technique he had been taught for obtaining one's desires. "Make a nonverbal symbol of what you desire," he advised me, "and put it out strongly, once, to the universe."

The next morning, sitting for my usual meditation, I tried to come up with a symbol of what I wanted. After some intense moments of attempting to enter blackness so there would be no mind-jabber to distract me, I saw my image: a spider web in a ring of gold. That was what I wanted—not so much a class as an atmosphere, an atmosphere which I could be in and hopefully create, with children.

The spider web stood for the spider's quiet absorption in the task at hand—a quality I lack. Spiders do not worry as they weave. They do not question or compare, grumble or doubt. A spider would not say, "Oh, I wove that other web so well, but it caught nothing. How do I know this one will work?" Nor would a spider bemoan the fact that another spider's web was prettier, or bigger. Spiders just *do*. I needed some of that spider *doing* now.

As for the ring of gold, that was the friendship, the love with which my class would be surrounded, with which it would surround itself. We would love ourselves, and out of that would come love for each other. It seemed to me that without that ring of gold, without that love, the spider web—and everything else in the world, for that matter— was useless. That ring of gold was you.

I surprised myself with the strength of my imaging. With more force than I knew I had, I put this image out, strongly projecting it, strongly asserting it to the universe. There was so much strength that I never asked myself, "Maybe it didn't work. Maybe I should do it again because the universe didn't get my message." I knew it had. And one week later I had my job.

In fact, toward the end of August I received two job offers, made within twenty-four hours of each other. The first job was as a teacher's aide in a private school. The second was as a sixth-grade teacher in a public school in Southborough, Massachusetts. I chose the second, knowing it would be more difficult. I wanted the challenge, the chance for creativity; and I also wanted the bonding that would come with having my own class. In other words, I wanted to create that atmosphere of a spider's web in a ring of gold.

I was so moved by this image—and by the efficacy of my prayer—that two days before school began, I took the time to *create* a spider's web in a ring of gold. I made a circular frame of copper wire, carefully wrapped thin gold thread around it, and then stretched black wool across the frame to form a web. This I hung from the ceiling of my classroom, a visible symbol. And all year long, whenever I found myself enmeshed in school anxieties—had we covered the material? Would my students do well on the standardized tests?—I would look up at this symbol to remember my purpose: absorption and love.

During the few days I had before the beginning of school, I made several small but fateful decisions. One was to clear a space for my class to sit in a circle on the floor. So strong was my belief in the power of a circle that I left a large area empty for that purpose, although it meant crowding the desks somewhat. Another decision was to arrange a trade with a neighboring teacher. He enjoyed teaching science most and asked if I would teach his class social studies and let him teach my class science. To be agreeable, I said yes, not knowing how costly this would prove to be.

When I began teaching, I had the belief, both innocent and outrageous, that all things were possible. A drawing done by a third grader of a rooster with a human haircomb on its head and the legend "Dare to be Different" expressed my attitude perfectly. With my naive confidence in the possibility of all things, totally unhampered by any sense of the conventional or any taste for normalcy, I plunged into the adventures of elementary school. I simply did not know the limits of public school teaching, and so I dared amazing things and, for a time, succeeded.

On the very first day of school, during the very first half

hour of class, I had us all sitting in a circle on the floor sharing a coconut. The coconut was a symbol of auspicious beginnings, according to a tradition of India. We smashed it open with a hammer—always an event of satisfying drama—and then shared the coconut meat. "Weird," my students later told me. "When we met you that first day, we thought you were really weird." As the year went on, there would be additions: "But we got to like you." "But we found out you were fun." And at the end my favorite, "And now you don't seem weird at all."

For many people the world is divided simply: Things are either weird or OK. Fortunately my students did not make this dichotomy. They tolerated my weirdness with good humor, which was just as well, since I gave them plenty to be tolerant about. In fact, right after we split the coconut for an auspicious beginning, I showed them how to do a breath count.

The breath count had a ten-year history behind it. It had begun when I began my intense pursuit of spiritual truths. After many years of perceiving "God" as an empty word, I was suddenly catapulted into an awareness that we humans are a lot bigger than we think and that there is an eternal rightness about what is happening now. The means was a mind-altering substance, and the result was twofold: I realized that understanding and recapturing this experience would be the aim of my life and that chemicals could have no further part in this.

Curiously enough, although there was no perception of God in that original experience, the sense of rightness somehow made the word "God" come alive; and I felt the company of God become a familiar part of my daily life. It surprised me how readily my two young children took to it all.

After years of no mention of God on my part, they immediately followed my suggestion that we talk out loud to God, which we would do at times when we were feeling particularly happy or grateful. And we began the custom of a blessing before meals.

As time went on, our spiritual paths became more carved out and defined. My son wanted a Hebrew blessing at mealtime, for we are Jewish. I preferred a chant connected with the meditation path I had found, which was working powerfully to keep me in contact with that eternal rightness and which, in fact, was watering my Jewish roots, sending me back to the old Hasidic tales with new delight in their wisdom.

For a while we experimented with spontaneous blessings and thanks. But as the children began to make more and more flowery speeches, extolling the mashed potatoes or the dessert to come, I realized this would not do. The solution was so simple: a breath count, which became our way for years.

Before each meal, we would all close our eyes and count five silent breaths, each person saying inside any words that might be chosen. When the five breaths were over, we would open our eyes, waiting for the last person to be done. Simple. Democratic. And amazingly satisfying. After protesting the mandatory silence for a while—having the giggles, laughing at burps, and so on, as children will do— my son and daughter began to enjoy their brief blessing. There is a special affection that rises when eyes are opening and each greets the other, coming out of the silence.

And so, my first morning in school, I introduced a breath count. I had done it many times as a substitute teacher and found that students were always interested, especially if we made a comparison of the normal and relaxed breathing rates. With my Southborough class the breath count evolved. We made it our object to come out of the count together, after about a minute and a half. We each had our own number of breaths, which we would adjust every week with the aim of finishing together.

Each morning we would sit in a circle on the floor, close our eyes, take our number of breaths, and wait for the last person to be done. For me it was a wonderful way to start the school day. Merely closing our eyes together was an act of trust. And I enjoyed watching the students emerge from the count. Not that I was able to watch all, for my count often put me in the middle. But I always felt a warm greeting for the ones I saw open their eyes—as if watching infants awaken or flowers open in a garden.

Not only did I initiate the breath count on that first day, but that first week I introduced what was to become our Friday relaxation. ("By Friday you need it!" Rona once commented, with the full wisdom of her eleven years. I agree.) Who would have believed that twenty-five sixth-graders' bodies could fit lying down on the floor of our public school classroom, all fully extended and most tucked carefully into the rows and spaces between the desks? And that we could actually get through a long (twenty to thirty minute) relaxation without being disturbed? But that is what we did.

We put signs on our three doors: "Please do not disturb. Relaxation in progress." We would turn off the lights, pull down the shades, and put on the tape recorder. The students would lie down on their backs and relax. They learned to relax deeply to music and to go into their imaginations. I would lead them in some guided imagery and eventually into their own silence.

"You are taking a walk in the woods," I would begin. "It is a warm day, but the trees are thick and the sunlight reaches you only in patches . . ." And off we would go, deep into the woods. Or we would go snorkeling at a coral reef. And once we took a bicycle ride along the beach. Our bicycles began to mount to the sky and we rode among the stars.

Some of the students got so quick at going into a deep relaxation that they asked for no talking at all, no imagery. But others began to fret—bored, they said, because nothing was happening. After many weeks I realized I would have to stop these whole-class relaxations because of those who fretted. I planned to make the relaxations optional, with an alternative activity elsewhere. But I never got to do that. My right to have a breath count and to have relaxations, even my right to sit on the floor in a circle with my class, turned out to be a privilege only, which was abruptly suspended.

But that is part of the story of the life and death of my class, and that is intertwined with the life and death of the baby, which is your story. And I am getting ahead of myself.

When school began in September, you were already present. If I had been more sharply aware, I could have sensed your presence. But it was my first time teaching and I thought the love was all my own.

How can I describe this love you filled me with, this love that was you, taking up residence, actually living in me? My eyes often got teary when I was speaking of my class and sometimes even when I was talking privately to one of my students. I was constantly praising my class, sometimes to the annoyance of my family. I drank my students in; I saw their beauty. They were good to each other, they were *nice*. For me this was the cardinal virtue. Without my even trying, they would provide me with the ring of gold.

That year has gone by now, and I look back with more clarity. Yes, I can see isolated instances of their treating each other poorly. But I maintain my original judgment. They *were* all nice, every single one of the twenty-five. There was not one who routinely fed on hurting another, not one who had the habit of attempting to feel better by making others feel worse. It seemed a miracle to me. I had seen all my own children's classes and had taught many a class as a substitute teacher, but I had never seen a class as nice as this one. Or was it just the glow you cast on them, and on me, too?

Of course it was not only a matter of their being nice to each other, which I tried to enhance, to expand slowly from niceness to caring to love. There were also my interactions with them. My love for my students could be found in the quiet intensity of these private exchanges.

I remember lovely Laura Lee, for example, beautiful inside and out, who burst into tears on the first day of school during a writing assignment. I spoke to her at recess. What was wrong? "I can't write," she sobbed, "I've never been able to and I never will. And it doesn't matter because I'm going to be a waitress like my mom." I saw how learning at school was tied into the deepest cosmic scripts for the children. Changes could be powerful. If I could free Laura's writing ability, I could free her confidence as well, give her a sense of choice in her own life.

Teaching was clearly giving. My only question was: Could I do it? I felt a sense of urgency. Could I hear what each soul was asking for underneath, and could I give it? I saw especially what a gift it would be to help my students learn to write about themselves. How many times did I hear them say in a dull voice, "I have nothing to write," or, "Nothing ever happens to me," or, "My life isn't interesting." I saw that most of the children felt that their lives were not storyful, not story-worthy. Helping them write about themselves would be getting them to see, perhaps even live, their lives in a new way.

I remember Hank very well. He had been kept back twice in school, in a series of moves from town to town, and was now two years older than his fellow sixth-graders. Two years? He was lifetimes older. He *saw*. He had a kind of clarity and distance that I have known only in adults. Some of the other teachers saw him as a tough kid and were wary around him. I saw him as a compatriot in consciousness. When there were discipline problems—and there were many—I never talked down to him. "You can't swear like that," I would tell him. "Most of the others in this class don't feel so imprisoned as you do. They're happier that way, they have some innocence. When you swear at assignments, you're taking that away from them." Though it may not have been intelligible by sixth-grade standards, I spoke to the highest in him, and it seemed he understood.

I was pleased to find that others in the class also learned to see through Hank's tough exterior of threats and snarls. Towards the end of the year I asked my students to pretend they were on a desert island where they would remain for the rest of their lives, to which they could invite one friend only, from class. To the sound of ocean surf on our tape recorder, they were to write a letter inviting that friend and explaining their choice. Hank received three invitations, the highest number of any boy. Students acknowledged his high energy and the fact that he was never fake.

Greg was the only challenge to my idea that everyone in class was nice. Normally a genial, perceptive child, Greg had spells of heartlessness. He had one the day we had our class picture taken. It must have been especially hard for him that day, for he was the only one in class who could not afford to buy a picture. That afternoon at recess I heard complaints: Greg was kicking people in the game. I called him over. His eyes were opaque. I tried to reach him, looked hard into his eyes for the light of human kindness, but found only inhuman black pinpoints. He explained coldly that he had the right to kick according to the rules of the game and that he was intentionally kicking to hurt.

It would have been normal to talk about playground rules. But I took the risk of skipping superficialities and went to first causes. "I know things are hard for you," I said, "with a new parent at home and not enough money to buy school pictures. Some people are given harder circumstances than others, and we don't always know why. Maybe it's to make them stronger, or to test how strong they are. Anyway, the point is, don't become less nice because things are difficult. That would just be one more loss, the worst one of all."

I was unsure whether this was a proper thing for a teacher to be saying, but I felt as if I were battling for a soul: I could not let that opaqueness remain. At some point Greg softened, tears filling his eyes and bringing the light back into them. "You're making me cry," he said. "Can I go downstairs and wash my eyes?" Perhaps I had gone too far, but I was acting out of love, not prudence. I felt so much love and concern for the children in my class: I wanted them to be their best, fullest, most beautiful selves.

I once read in a children's book about "naming" others, which means seeing the best and speaking to that best in them, thereby calling it forth. This is what I did with my students. In other years, I had to try hard to "name" all the children I worked with. It took work to overlook the aggressiveness and nastiness I sometimes saw in them or, harder yet, to understand it as part of their life's learning pattern. But with the students of my class now, the "naming" was effortless and natural: I simply loved them all.

This love for my students was not pure. It was mixed with fear of failure. When I robbed our home of interesting objects to make my class a better place, I did it out of fear of failure. And when, worse yet, I robbed our home of my attention and smiles because I was preoccupied going over my students' written papers or planning more, I did it out of fear of failure. But my family thought I did it out of love, and they were hurt. It seemed to them—to Michael, my husband, to Elena, my twelve-year-old daughter, and to Joshua, my fifteen-year-old son—that I was putting the welfare of my class over their own.

September passed. Like most first-year teachers, I spent almost all my waking hours on preparations and still managed to feel unsure on most school days, as if I were continually in the process of falling off a cliff. By the beginning of October I was just beginning to gather confidence.

I remember especially the first weekend of October. Less than half a mile from our house was a beautiful domed structure, known as the Dome of Peace, built by Japanese Buddhist monks and volunteers from the United States and abroad. The Dome had just been completed, and this was the weekend of its inauguration ceremony. The immense, closed dome would house a relic of the Buddha in a sealed chamber, and its purpose was to draw peace to our troubled planet. There were over eighty such domes all over the world, and this one was the first to be completed in our country.

Michael and I had taken part in building the Dome of Peace, and we had affection and respect for both the structure itself and the group who built it, whom we called simply "the Buddhists." We had met the Buddhists a year and a half earlier, by coincidence on the very first day they began working on their land. It was a snowy spring day, and we were taking a walk in the woods. To our surprise, we found a small clearing and some people who were attempting to drag the trunk of a huge felled tree, with the help of an amazing medieval-looking wooden winch. In the distance, shouting directions in a language we could not understand, was a small Asian man who could have been cast in a movie as a peasant. Two American women were leaning into the wheel, but did not have the strength to turn it. So we pushed with them, and the tree was cleared. And from that day on we were connected with their structure, as it slowly rose.

The winch, we later learned, was called a *mandiki*, which means "power of a thousand," the land was being cleared for the Dome of Peace, and the peasant was none other than the head monk. Soon after our first meeting, we had had three Buddhist monks sleeping at our house for the summer, and we invited the entire crew of workers over for dinner on several evenings. We supplied water to fill their tanks, and showers for those in need, and also we helped with construction work on the Dome itself.

It was a privilege to watch the Dome rise, for we knew the

dedication that went into it. Labor was voluntary, skills were learned on the spot, and equipment was homemade. The Buddhists themselves were an extraordinary group. As I came to know them, I found that they were incredibly "large"—I know no other way to say it. So many of them were living with great joy, energy, and abandon. They had dedicated their summer or their year, and some of them their lives, to the practices taught by their teacher: building domes the world over, bowing to the Buddha nature in all beings, and chanting the mystic seven syllables which they believed would bring world peace. I had seen other individuals of their stature, but never a whole group.

On the weekend of the inauguration of the Dome of Peace, we had guests at our house who had come for the festivities. But I had pitifully little time to spend with them. Except for attending the inauguration itself, I was almost always sitting on the dining room floor preparing for school, surrounded by my papers and my books.

I was embarrassed at having so little time to spend with our guests and sorry to have so little energy for helping with the ceremony. But at least my policy of constant preparation seemed to be working. The Monday after the inauguration, for the first time ever, I knew what I was doing at school every second of the day. And Tuesday I continued that way, relaxed and at leisure, confident in my plans.

I came home from school that second Tuesday in October feeling like a normal teacher for the first time in my life. Now I understood how teachers could survive the school year, and even dared to hope I might survive until summer.

I have suspected for many years that a certain pattern operates in my life: It seems that the minute I master anything, the rug is always pulled out from under me and the situation changes. I certainly had not mastered elementary school teaching, but perhaps I was close enough. Because the rug was certainly pulled.

Five weeks into school, I had become aware that my monthly cycle was not what it should be. All summer long it had been troublesome, showing up late and briefly, but now it seemed to have completely disappeared. Was I sick? Having early menopause? I made an appointment with the doctor. "You might as well have a pregnancy test," Michael cautioned. "Otherwise the doctors will just say they can't make any diagnosis until they rule out pregnancy." Pregnancy, I knew, was impossible. Our combination of methods had worked for fifteen years. But just to avoid delay, I went in for a pregnancy test before my appointment.

I had taken the test on the Monday after the inauguration of the Dome of Peace and forgotten about it completely. And now, coming home on Tuesday, sinking in the sofa cushions, feeling the relaxation of my second normal day of teaching, I heard the telephone ring. It was the nurse from the medical center. "Mrs. Saffire," she said, "we have your test results, and they are positive."

Pregnant! I was completely stunned. When? How? We used precautions; it was impossible. The surge of power. For a moment the picture flashed before me: my enemy lying broken to bits in the waters of my tide, like the pieces of a Hopi kachina doll. That had to be it. But that was impossible!

Except for the shock of disbelief, which passed in a moment, I had only one other feeling: joy, an immediate and clear joy. I had not wanted a child, and yet the joy was unmistakable. It seemed to be simply a pure joy at life, at the new life in me. I telephoned Michael to tell him the news. He expressed no surprise or disbelief, but he did react with the very same joy. We were proving the observation of the poet William Blake: "For all that lives is holy. Life delights in life."

I hung up the phone and, like an amateur Sherlock Holmes, raced to my journal, keen for clues. Surely there would be evidence of the pregnancy in it. I turned some pages. Aha! There it was, our August vacation on Block Island: "My stomach has been in smithereens. So often a bitter metallic taste after dinner." I paged further back, to July. The clay poultices! I had had some painful breast swelling in July and decided to test at last the healing power of clay. For days I sat in the sun with the gooey green clay hardening on my breasts. I thought I had disproved the poultice theory when the swelling didn't go away. But now I saw: I was pregnant. That clay never had a chance.

I paged further back in the journal. Where was the vision of my ocean tides and the broken doll? I kept turning the pages. Ah, there it was: June 17. It was now October 8, almost four months later. Could I really have failed to notice a pregnancy for four months?

Intrepid record keeper that I am, I had a special folder for recording the variables of my monthly cycle so that I could know just when to expect a chocolate craving, euphoria, uncaused agitation, and so on. I checked the dates. Yes, June 17 would have been one of the two or three days of the month when we would have made love without any precaution other than the timing itself. But that is because it was absolutely impossible for me to conceive on that day. I know.

And now, I am able to say that I was beginning to come into an awareness of your visit. Oh, it was not full awareness. It was never full until after you had come and gone. But already there were hints. I knew this was no normal pregnancy.

First of all there was the impossibility of the conception. I had no evidence of the June 17 date, which was later confirmed by ultrasound. But if it *was* June 17, and I felt sure it was, then I knew this was a miracle—something as close to an immaculate conception as I would ever get. I knew no one would believe me. And I could picture people shaking their heads in disbelief, thinking, "Another casualty of the rhythm method." But I was sure that this was an impossible conception.

Furthermore I felt it was significant that the pregnancy had been kept hidden from me for so long. Why you chose to hide yourself I did not know. But I am an intelligent and observant person. I knew it was no accident that I had not realized I was pregnant for almost four months.

At this point I had come to only two conclusions: The pregnancy was impossible, and the masking of it unlikely. And from the impossibility of the pregnancy I deduced a third: Since I had not chosen you, you must have chosen me. An image from memory kept coming back to confirm my sense of having been chosen. And this was the beginning of my recognition of our true relationship.

Years earlier I had gone to pick a puppy out of a litter of eight. I thought I had a clever scheme: I had brought eight loops of differently colored yarn and pencil and paper. I was going to put a loop around the neck of each puppy and then observe as the puppies played, taking notes on their qualities and antics to decide which one to choose. It never got that far. The third puppy bit the yarn as I tried to put it around her neck and would not let go. We tussled for about five minutes. I tugged and she tugged back, pulling her head away, but occasionally looking sideways at me with glistening eyes and a winsome glance. Finally I took it as a sign. I thought I was choosing a puppy, but it was she who had chosen me.

I was relieved that it was the puppy who had made the choice. After all, she was in touch with her natural instincts, while I would have been using reason, trying to balance my preferences and observations. So now with this pregnancy, I felt the same sort of trust and relief. Had I decided in June to have a child, I would have suspected my motives: Was I just yielding to a blind desire to make more me's? Or acting out of fear, needing to fill my time lest I not get a job? But now, feeling chosen, I trusted: The one who chose me must know what it was doing. And whenever I would think about the pregnancy, the image would come to me of this tiny golden retriever puppy holding the brightly colored yarn in her teeth.

Much later, when the pregnancy became known, I shared the story of the puppy with my class, telling them how I had felt chosen. Laura Lee must have pondered this story the rest of the year. For on the last day of school, during the last minutes of our final recess, she blurted out her question: "Mrs. Saffire, remember when you were pregnant and you said the baby chose you? Well how could it? How could there *be* a baby already that could choose you?"

What a profound question! For a moment I flashed back to that beautiful verse of the *Bhagavad Gita*, about how the soul puts on and takes off these selves of ours like so many overcoats. I gave it a try, knowing it was hopeless. "Well," I questioned her, "when you go into a store to buy a coat, don't you have to exist first so you can choose the coat?" Yes, she followed that. "Well then," I continued, "maybe the soul of a baby decides to put on a body the way we decide to put on a coat."

Laura Lee took this in, chewed it, and then spit it out with a protest: "But with the coat it's different. The coat *does* exist before you go to buy it, but how could the baby exist before it has a body?"

"Well," I said, nodding mysteriously, "maybe it can. Who knows?" Our time was up. I smiled and let it go at that. I knew Laura Lee had not had her question answered, but inside I was smiling still. "Ah, Laura Lee," I was thinking, "what a true philosopher you are. I'm sorry I couldn't answer your question. But never mind. Just sitting with that question is an education in itself."

After the phone call I slipped into the new reality: I was pregnant. The moment I heard I was pregnant, it was so obvious. Michael and I laughed to see. How could we have doubted it? My breasts were swollen, my belly seemed enormous. No wonder I had not been able to fit into the three pairs of slacks I had bought last June!

We decided to tell no one except our children. It seemed that pregnancy at my age was a risky thing. And I felt especially uneasy seeing how my body had masked the signs of pregnancy, with my monthly cycle apparently continuing for so long. (Doctors assured me that this was not a bad sign. But I later read in one medical book that it was.) There was no point making my students fear the loss of their new teacher when a pregnancy was so uncertain.

I was torn at the thought of leaving my class; I knew it would distress them. Or perhaps I was projecting, knowing only how much it would distress me to leave them. In particular I worried for Eddy, who was severely depressed over his father's death a year ago. Some days he would sit staring, almost motionless, for half an hour at a time. Once when I suggested that he just put pen in hand and make himself write anything on the paper, no matter what, he looked at me sadly and said, "I tell my hand to write, but it won't." How could I leave him now? He would feel doubly abandoned. I did not want to leave my class at all.

There was also the question of amniocentesis, to test for Down's syndrome. At my age the statistical chance of having a baby with Down's syndrome was one in forty, and there was a Down's syndrome child among my relatives. I did not know what we would do if this was our situation. I had gone the route of abortion once, years earlier—before the word "God" had any resonance for me and before I had an idea of the yogi's courage to take all life offers as a gift—and I did not think I could go that route again. Also, we now practiced nonviolence. Michael would catch our attic mice in live traps and we would release them into distant fields. (Forty-one in one winter!) And I would capture wasps and spiders in a jar, to escort them outside and carefully release them. The only exception was my apologetic execution of the fleas found on my dog. No, I thought, no matter what the result of the tests, killing we could not do.

But what about disinviting? I had heard of a doctor in Arizona who advised patients to disinvite unwanted babies, with amazing results. Time after time, after the mother regretfully requested the soul to leave because the time was not right, there would be a spontaneous end to the pregnancy, a miscarriage within three days. Might I disinvite the baby if it had Down's syndrome? Michael and I discussed this at length. Was it not violent also? Was this not killing, only on a subtler level? No, it did not quite feel that way. Given our uncertainty, we arranged for amniocentesis. It would be weeks before we would learn the results. Until then, we would tell no one.

There followed a period of concealment. I found the concealment difficult, for I have always been extremely open, without the normal boundaries of privacy or shame. But I made it a challenge, a test of my ability to control my mind. During the school day I simply legislated the pregnancy out of my "field"—out of the atmosphere of thoughts and feelings that surrounded me. Every once in a while, though, especially when the classroom was unruly, I would remember my secret, checking inwardly: "Is this a good environment for a baby to grow in? Are the vibrations in this room healthy enough, is there enough love?" To my surprise, the answer I received was always "yes."

I told Diane, the principal, my news when requesting a day off for amniocentesis. I said I had not had any idea that I was pregnant when I began teaching, and that I expected to leave school at the end of February, just before the baby was due. I was delighted at Diane's reaction. Although my leaving would give her the burden of finding a replacement at midyear, she simply shared in my joy, without a trace of regret.

I told the superintendent also, who wandered into my classroom one day while my students were in the gym. With tears in my eyes, I announced I would be leaving. I told him that as long as finances permitted, and they did, I would stay home for the first years to take care of any child who had chosen me for mother. These two I told; but from all others I kept my news a secret.

There was only one time I came close to giving the game away. I had to choose my clothes carefully. Since no slacks closed around my waist, I had to hide my waistline, which I usually did with loose button-down sweaters. But one day, towards the end of the concealment, I dared to wear a risky overblouse, one that would make me look pregnant at any time. I saw some girls on the playground whispering during my recess duty and pointing at me. Feeling adventurous I asked them what was up. "Are you pregnant?" one of them asked, giggling. They had guessed! I hate lying and avoid it at all costs. Now I was stumped: What could I say? I laughed gaily. "I'd never tell anyone if I were." True enough. The rumor stopped right there.

And then there was that day, again towards the very end of the concealment, when even the last snap of the three wouldn't stay shut on my slacks. We were sitting in a circle on the floor, and the floor-sitting position was too much of a strain. I must have heard that last snap pop open and re-closed it seven times. "How am I going to get away with this?" I wondered. But no one said anything. Later, when I revealed the pregnancy to my students, I asked Jonathan, who had been sitting next to me that day, "Do you remember that day when my snap kept opening? I thought I could never stay in hiding." He did! We laughed and laughed together.

There was concealment from others, but also from ourselves. Michael and I simply never let ourselves feel the practical concerns of having a child. It was curious to me: With the two children I already had, I felt an enormous sense of responsiblity, because we had chosen to bring them into the world. But with this child, who had chosen us, I felt absolved of all responsibility. Yes, the bomb might fall and the quality of life seemed to be diminishing. But surely this soul, with its vantage point from outer dimension, knew that better than I. If it had foreseen all that and chosen us anyway, who was I to worry?

Also strange to me, the everyday details of having a child never seemed real. With our other children there were the questions of what to name them, how to set up a room for them, and so on. But with this pregnancy Michael and I never pictured the mundane everyday realities except to laugh at them. Every once in a while, for fun, we would "pinch" ourselves mentally with a reminder. "Changing diapers!" one of us would call out. "Parent-teacher meetings at school!" the other would counter. These phrases became the punch lines of a single joke, for us hilarious. "Watching kids' softball games!" Michael would intone in mock agony, and we would roll our eyes and start laughing. And I remember once, as we drove somewhere, I turned to him and asked, "What about those early birthday parties?" "Oh no!" he moaned, and we laughed together again.

But we never took any of this seriously. The diapers were not real, the birthday parties were not real. We never thought about braces or saving for a college education. Perhaps we were simply holding all these thoughts in until the results of the amniocentesis came. Or perhaps we already knew inside what was going to be.

As we were later told, you never intended to have a childhood with us.

Slowly my ideas about you came into focus. I knew from the beginning that I had been chosen by you. And a second fact, most mysterious, I learned soon after: I could not find you in the baby's body. I am in the habit of consulting and calling on all sorts of things, animate and inanimate. "Car keys, where are you?" Or, to a hapless attic mouse being left off in a field, separated from its winter cache, "I wish you well. Be brave. Robinson Crusoe could do it, and so can you." And so, of course, I called on you and tried to probe your being.

I would use my radar, especially during meditation when my mind was quietest, and scan for a soul. "Baby, are you there? You who have chosen us, are you with me right now?" I would become as still and receptive as I could. But almost never was there even a remote sense of presence. Even when I was lying in bed at night and could feel that tiny body kicking, I would ask and feel no response.

I had thoughts and theories to explain your absence. I knew that according to certain belief systems of India, the soul of an infant enters only at the fourth or fifth month. And I wondered whether this might explain your absence (and also assuage misgivings over my past abortion). But I knew that you were able to make your presence felt. After all, you had announced yourself already once, in the form of ocean power.

I had read in one book that although the soul makes its engagement with a human body from the beginning, it is free to roam around at will, and many souls prefer to stay away from the body as long as they can, reentering only at birth. This made sense to me. I knew that if I had the choice, I would rather stay out zooming around in space—a sort of firefly existence, as I imagined it—rather than confine myself to a physical form in a dark and salty womb. Even so, I wondered why there was not at least a visit now and then. With my daughter, who was born close to the time that my intuition opened up, I sensed ahead that I would give birth to a dark-haired girl, and so it happened. But with you, there was not enough presence for me to know even that.

I would call for you and feel the baby's form inside me, knowing that you could locate yourself there if you chose. But when I checked that tiny, growing form, I found no inhabitant. That form seemed to me an empty chair. Chair?

Throne, I say now, now that I know you better, know your greatness. A throne for a queen was being constructed— slowly, painstakingly, with additions and refinements every day, a perfect throne waiting to be occupied in perfection.

Perhaps I was scanning with the wrong radar and that is why I could not find you. After all, I was looking for a human soul. I was looking for something like the seedlike concentration of desires, qualities, and lessons to be learned, which is my own driving force. I expected to find a being who had chosen me and my family as the supporting cast in the next scene of its learning drama, a being who was either forced into human existence by the necessity of further learning or who was lured here by the promise of pleasure. If I was looking for that, I could scarcely have found you.

But also, I think, you did not choose to appear to me as other. You lived in me as my love for my class, and you would live in me as my love for my husband, and you would be the taskmaster of the most difficult and subtle test of my life. But you did not choose to meet me face to face, in the fullness of your nature. Not yet.

It is tempting to speak of you as if you were the visitor in my womb, and yet I know this cannot be. In some sense you *were* that tiny baby, that lovely infant girl whose brief life graced my own. But in another sense you were not. It seems absurd to me, impossible, to give a date for your conception, or to delimit the span of a lifetime for you. You simply do not exist in time. You are eternal; that much I know. You borrowed a form, yes, which *did* exist in time. But that form was just your chariot, your throne.

So then, who are you? I call you my Golden Lady. But what do you call yourself? What are you, really? Are you goddess, or guide, or both? Are you an angel? Who or what are you in the fullest expanse of your being?

I once strained hard when I seemed to be in a state of consciousness that would let me reach you. I thought I caught a glimpse—a sense of verticality and gold. Long vertical lines like the folds of a toga. And shining gold, almost gaudy, bright as gilding on the folds' ridges. But was that you? I asked for a name, and seemed to hear one. But when I called that name, it did not summon the golden quality of your love, but rather brought a disturbing state of double-mindedness, where I felt a coming and a going at once.

Who are you, then? I have refined my ideas of who you are not. But can I say who you are? My ideas of you have grown so slowly, ever since the birth. Months go by and one clue is thrown to me, and then, months later, another. I can say this for sure: that you are eternal and that this baby, which you did inhabit fully once and only once, did not exhaust even the smallest fraction of your existence.

I remember the birth (I dare not say *your* birth) perfectly: that tiny form, that perfect, smooth, and delicate girl's form, so tiny it would barely have filled a shoebox. But your presence so enormous. You filled the room, permeated it to every corner. And people filed into the room, drawn by your presence. The pretense was medical, I realize. But the inner eye knows when it sees people kneeling to the holy.

The baby was you, yes. She drew her waters from the well of your existence. But you were not the baby, could not be confined to that baby or to any other form. I know with all my being that you spent but a penny's worth of your existence on that lovely baby girl. And yet that penny's worth enriched me beyond measure.

~

Always I have been struck by Rilke's line: *wann wendet er an unser Sein die Erde und die Sterne?* "When does God spend on our existence the earth and stars?" Now I had my answer. Yes, normally God spent on me as on others: the small blessings and pleasures that make up the miracle of ordinary life. But this day, in these few hours, the universe poured forth its gifts. You filled that room, permeated it with the vibrance of your presence, and all things were in that: the stars and the earth, time and timelessness, love and (ah! so loving) death.

And so I wrestle. I try hard to reach you, to muster an understanding that will match my longing. I saturate my mind with thoughts that reach out towards you, until I can hold no more. Then I attempt to wring out understanding from my mind, like water from a sponge. There is longing, there is love, there is effort, there is pain. This is the hardest work I do. And still I know you not. Will I ever truly know you?

*D*arshan. This mysterious word from India sums you up.
It was my window to you in those early days of pregnancy,
my one true way of seeing you, although I did not know it
then. The word literally means "seeing;" nothing mysterious about that. But it is used for being in the company of a
saint or master—someone whose power can pull one in-
stantly into a sea of love or silence—and, oh, what a mystery there is to that!

Michael and I had learned of darshan by being with our meditation teacher, who was from India. The word brings back to me the hall where he sat and the line—called the darshan line—of hundreds, thousands on holidays, who slowly stepped forward to receive his touch. The transaction lasted only moments but its effect was profound. I would watch people come up looking pinched and leave looking open, come up looking hungry and leave looking fed. For the darshan of this man my family had gone to California, where we lived for four months in a room at his ashram.

So many feelings as I stood on that long line inching slowly toward him. "I am naked," I would think from far away. "This is the final judgment after death, when I shall be reviewed for what I really am. I can hide nothing from this man." And there would be both excitement and a curious relief—that at last I could stop posturing. Or, coming close to him, I might take in a sudden breath of intoxication, as if inhaling that first exhilarating whiff of salty breeze when coming near the ocean. And finally, I would be standing just before him, feeling total stillness, as if in a dark cave, unopened for thousands of years.

To experience this sort of darshan even once is to realize that the word is needed; for darshan becomes something which one revisits in memory and longs to find again. And so the word became a part of our vocabulary. At first we reserved it for the strong darshan of a master, but gradually we extended our use of the term for any moment of intense connection. We found that when people love each other, the magic of that love can pierce the heart and bring darshan. At first I noticed this with family and friends. But as time went on, I sensed it happening with people I barely knew, even with animals or plants: rare moments when being with another suddenly burst into flower, a wordless communication, essence to essence.

It was the latter sort of darshan which I expected with you. I was wrong, of course. I thought of you then as a limited individual, like ourselves. And so I thought that you had come to share darshan with us, to give us yours and partake of ours. Now that I know you better, know more of who you are, I realize it was not a trade and never could have been. Like my meditation teacher, like all the saints of history, like the beings of our dreams and visions, who touch us on the shoulder and say, "Go now, you are healed," you would come, once, radiant with yourself. And that would be your darshan.

It did not surprise me that a soul would seek my family out for darshan. After all, every year more than a thousand students at the local university have taken my husband's course, and he has had to turn down hundreds more. Students bring their sisters and brothers, mothers and lovers. Having come to his lectures, I know the atmosphere he creates: His words are slow, his logic clear, and there is the punctuation of extraordinary bursts of humor; but most of all, there is peace. It slows a person down—slows down the thoughts and gives rest from mental wandering—just to sit and listen to him talk. One of his students, waking late one morning and realizing she had turned off her alarm clock in her sleep, cried at having missed his lecture. Another faithfully attended his course though she had taken it the semester before. When asked why, she answered, "It keeps me sane."

If Michael was sought after as a professor, I would expect him to be sought after as a father even more. For this is a role he has filled surpassingly. His physical energy has always been extreme. When the children were small, he would often be found throwing them up in the air or blowing on their bellies for a tickle. And when they grew, there was the everlasting offer of a baseball game or a tickling-wrestling match. His playfulness was yet another gift. If a child asked for a piece of bread with dinner, Michael would go to the kitchen and come back with a mournful expression on his face, as if there were none left—then suddenly lift his arm and shake the bread out of his sleeve with a great big, sparkling smile. He was always there for all the little services, gladly packing the special snack for lunch or helping with homework. The pregnancy caused me to look at him with renewed appreciation.

And at my daughter, too. Joshua, my son, was not so interested in the baby, regarding the newcomer as a stranger he would barely get to know before leaving for college in two years' time. But Elena's attitude was warm and welcoming from the beginning. Sometimes I felt as if the baby were coming to meet her. In fact the thought was so strong that I wondered at times if I would die in childbirth and Elena would be the baby's mother. I knew that she could do it, for she is both responsible and nurturing. And she has shown herself a powerhouse of love from her earliest years.

I remember how, when she was two years old, I would come in to her room to give her a good-night hug and, hugging her, feel myself surrounded by her arms and by her love. I felt her bigger than myself, as if she were the mother and I the child. This happened so often that I had ample chance for scrutiny. In the middle of a hug I would recognize the familiar feeling, marvel, check to see if it could really be so, and yes, find myself still bathing in that enormous sea of love.

Someone once asked me about Elena and I answered, to my own surprise, "She was my first teacher of love." It is true that I needed the years of watching Michael's steady giving. But for some reason I could not learn from him how to give love fully, although I tried. It was when Elena was born that I first learned to open myself up and let love flood through.

Immodest as it was, it seemed to me that any soul who came to share in darshan with Michael and Elena was showing good taste. And to my happiness, I included myself in their number. For the first time in my life I could understand why a soul might seek me out for company. The pregnancy allowed me to revise my self-assessment: a welcome change.

I had been selfish and self-centered as a child and had not outgrown those traits as easily as others seem to do. And so, from childhood on, I carried with me the subconscious sense of dislike, by self and others, which selfishness brings with it. It had taken me a long time to lose that selfishness and become what I think of as, simply, nice. I had to struggle hard and suffer much to acquire the simple niceness that others seem to come by naturally. I would try not to feel smug. But somewhere inside me was the feeling that goes with the phrase "a self-made man," as if I had earned every penny of niceness on my own.

And now, this year, it seemed to me that finally I was not only nice, but loving. After years of watching the example of my husband, and with the coaching of my daughter, I felt that I had finished the course and flowered into love myself. Perhaps the love I felt this year was a gift, your presence in me yet unknown. All I know is that it felt to me as if I had at last a fully human heart.

School days passed without event. It was when I was with Michael, away from school, that I fully experienced the initial period of pregnancy.

I remember one early day of magic when we went mountain climbing, four days after we received the news that I was pregnant. My parents had planned to come up for a weekend visit, and Michael and I decided to take this opportunity, perhaps our last for years, to go away together. I thought of my parents as "professional worriers," likely to envision countless mishaps and urge me to take precautions against every single one. And so, much as I wanted to, we did not share our news with them.

I had not yet learned how to dress in a discreet but comfortable way, and I remember my sigh of relief as we pulled out of the driveway. At last I could unsnap my slacks! But also I had not yet learned to legislate the pregnancy out of my field with ease. And my relief was even greater at being able again to express myself naturally, to speak without passing each remark through the filter of concealment.

We drove a few hours and took a motel room, where I changed into my baggy overall dungarees. We packed our sandwiches, drove a bit more, and started up the mountain. It was a beautiful day in the early fall. We decided not to go straight to the top, but to visit a side spur first, a lovely grass-topped knoll, with low bushes and a distant view. We rested there and moved on. Never have I been so sleepy climbing. Perhaps it was the pregnancy. I know only that I yawned audibly as we climbed, and I yawned in the middle of my own conversation.

The ground was rocky everywhere. But between the spur and the peak we had found one little spot of soft grass between two giant crags. Michael climbed a crag while I lay down on the grassy spot, in a patch of sunlight. I felt my own radiance and fell into a blessed sleep.

The sleep was magical. This was, I suppose, the Madonna hour of the early pregnancy. I cannot say that this was you, although it may have been. I know that I have seen this face of human existence, this pure light of maternity, in my other pregnancies and in other pregnant women as well.

The glow was there, but what set this hour apart was that I could sense Michael's participation. It was as if I were both myself and he at once. I was below, napping, but also I was elsewhere, able to look down on myself and see the light that I was bathing in. I was aware, too, of Michael looking down and aware of his awareness of the light. I cannot say whether I was in both of us at once, or whether I was elsewhere, above, diffuse as the air, aware of all.

I awoke to the perfection of all things. Michael and I compared notes. He had gone to leap from one crag to another, over a drop of about ten feet. He was about to make the leap, he said, when he looked down on me. He realized that he could not take the risk, not with a baby on the way who would need years of caring and carrying. Was he disappointed, resentful? He checked his own feelings: no, he accepted it in the gentlest way.

He saw a radiant beauty in me as I slept, and kept his eyes on me the entire time. Looking at my sleeping form, he felt love and protectiveness. It was an outpouring of the tenderness that had been growing in these past four days. (Four days only? How many worlds we lived, and in so short a time. Well, that was all the time we had.) Never bored, he continued to watch, guarding me in his heart and marveling at what he saw.

Six days after the climb we went for the amniocentesis.
After filling out forms and undergoing routine counseling,
we went in for the procedure. The doctor's needle was long
and scary. Did I feel fear? I examined my feelings. No, what
I was feeling was actually the expectation of fear, based on
all the memory traces of other painful experiences with a
doctor's needle. But in fact I was calm and would remain so
the entire time. I would use mantra to maintain my calm, to
protect the baby and myself.

Mantra was my area of competence. I had been given a Sanskrit mantra by my meditation teacher years earlier and had gone through so many stages of its use. In the beginning, I thought that this mantra would save me—would literally save me from all pain and fear, would tear me from the merry-go-round of death and rebirth. I went through a period of intense determination to repeat the mantra inwardly at all times, which was also a period of constant self-abuse. For whenever I would start to repeat the mantra, I would first give myself a mental slap because I had not been saying it all along.

Eventually a saner policy evolved. Somewhere along the way I lost my belief that the mantra would be my path to salvation, and I lost my ambition to use it full time. But I found that sometimes the mantra arose spontaneously, and other times it was there for me, a ready tool in my pocket, to be used at will, especially in situations where direct action would be of no avail. When my son's friend fell playing hockey on the ice, for example, and we were sitting together waiting to find out whether he had a concussion, I felt mantra flowing silently from myself to him. Or at the dentist's, when having x-rays, I would say mantra inwardly to prevent the scatter of those damaging rays, knowing that at best it would protect me and at least would calm my mind.

So now, in the doctor's office, I used the mantra to protect myself from fear of the needle, and also to protect the baby from being harmed by either the needle or the ultrasound vibrations. The doctor pointed out features of the tiny form on the screen. Although I had accepted the reality of the pregnancy long before, it still amazed me to see the baby's form. Judging by its size, the doctor confirmed the June 17 conception. I was not really surprised. I had just enough presence of mind to register a brief "Ah, I always knew." But already my mind was elsewhere, focused on the mantra.

Om namah shivaya, om namah shivaya. "I bow to Shiva." I remember how, when I first learned this mantra, I thought it was sacred and therefore secret. But on a trip to India, I found that it was widely known and used. Even my taxi driver had it printed on his dashboard. (And he showed a fine Shiva-like disregard for life, I noticed, as he raced around Bombay!) Who was this Shiva to whom I bowed? For me, this Shiva was not the fearsome god with the blue throat and the trident, and not even the dancer, with his four arms. Shiva was simply pure being, that Being out of which all existing things are made. Others might think it idolatrous to bow to Shiva. To me it was the most obvious posture in the world. Who does not bow in awe at the incredible carnival of existence all around and at its source?

Om namah shivaya, om namah shivaya. Once on the inbreath, and once on the outbreath. "I bow to the one who is pure Being, and to the one who has put on the infinite disguises of the many things that are. I bow to the one who is eternally, to the one we really are."

Om namah shivaya. As I mentally hummed my obeisance to all that is, I was also addressing the baby. "Whoever you are, I will take care of you, I will protect you." With my other two children, I so often felt like a little girl dressed up in the high heels of motherhood, surprised to find myself the one making snap decisions or keeping up standards of behavior in an impossibly grown-up way. But on this day I was truly in command. I was truly feeling a mother's calm and competence.

Om namah shivaya. "Baby, whoever you are, I am building a wall of syllables around you. Do not worry. The needle will not hurt you, and the ultrasound rays will not hurt you either. Just as the walls of my belly are holding you in to protect you, so also the walls of these syllables will keep you from harm."

It would be three weeks later that the results of the amniocentesis were phoned in: Everything was normal.
Michael took the call, and cried.

The last magic day of the early, unclouded period of pregnancy was a day of strong darshan, not yours, but the kind that one day I would recognize as yours.

It was four days before the amniocentesis results would be phoned in. But on this day we felt absolutely positive that the baby was in good health. Perhaps this was simply because our own hearts were high with pleasure and anticipation. It was a dazzling autumn day, the kind that makes living in New England unquestionably worthwhile. The sky was clear and blue; the leaves were turning color brilliantly. And there was that crispness in the air that I learned to love by leaving New England and living through a year without it. We were on our way to New Hampshire, to visit our friend, Caroline.

Caroline is a channel for a guide named Genesis, who speaks through her when she is in a trance. When I first met her a year and a half earlier and learned she was a channel, I was wary. I was firmly rooted in the belief that human life is for human living, and that one had better not have any truck with nonhuman entities. An old Hasidic story summed up my feeling exactly:

One day a rabbi was walking in the woods with his disciple, and the birds were singing. "Ah," sighed the disciple, "wouldn't it be wonderful to understand the language of the birds!" The rabbi answered with earthy good humor: "And you," he asked, "what you yourself are saying you already understand?" Just so, I felt about myself. It seemed to me it would be a full-time occupation simply to understand what I was about in this life, and I had no interest in what I considered sidelines: knowing past lives, speaking with nonhuman entities, or anything of the sort.

But I had a puzzling medical problem, which I felt unable to solve through Western medicine, and that eventually led me, one day when Caroline was at our house, to ask if I could consult Genesis about it. The result was something beyond my expectation: I did get an answer to my medical question. But what overwhelmed me was the feeling of darshan I had in the presence of Genesis.

By the time I met Genesis, my meditation teacher had been dead for two years. I had lost not only his darshan but also the wholeness of my faith in him, and I was in an unacknowledged mourning over both losses. Being with him had been in some ways the sweetest experience of my life, one I expected never to have again. There is a famous story about a population of geometric figures living in a land of only two dimensions. They could bump into each other and make contact at their outlines, but they could never touch or be touched on their insides. One day a three-dimensional visitor came and, from his position above, he could touch them on their insides. Imagine what a powerful experience that must have been for them! The same was my experience with my meditation teacher: He touched me in a place where I had not been touched before.

When Genesis spoke to me, I felt myself again in the presence of my teacher, touched on the inside. And Michael, who spoke separately with Genesis, felt it, too. Hearing Genesis speak, I experienced a return of reverence; and something sealed inside me was reopened.

As with my meditation teacher, I was in such awe of Genesis that I could not bring myself to ask for favors. And so I never asked Caroline if I could speak with him again, although I must have always hoped. During the intervening months we met Caroline several times, usually at a restaurant midway between her house and ours. And now, on this beautiful autumn day, one year since we first met Genesis, we were invited to her house.

We had a cozy breakfast in the kitchen, chatting over all sorts of things. I remember Caroline's mentioning that the soul of the baby was probably a "merry old soul" who had come to visit us, "old soul" being common parlance in some circles for one who has lived many lifetimes and become spiritually mature—and I knew that "Old King Cole" would never sound the same! After breakfast we moved into the dining room, and Caroline asked if we would like to speak with Genesis. We responded with a heartfelt yes, and turned on a tape recorder to preserve his words, which we would find precious.

When Caroline channels, there are no grand physical changes. She simply sits quietly for about half a minute, cocks her head almost quizzically to one side, and begins to speak. Her voice has its normal pitch and timbre, but the pronunciation is different. And the courtesy, the particular quality of courtliness, is Genesis' own.

Genesis greeted us, using Caroline's voice, and confirmed that all was fine with us and that we had an exciting year ahead. He gave Michael an exercise in meditation, which he said I could practice too. We were to use the imagery of a corridor. As we sat to meditate, we were to visualize ourselves walking down a corridor towards a door. We were to count to ten mentally and go through that door, leaving our physical selves behind; then, counting another ten slow paces, we were to go through the next door, this time losing our thoughts, our sense of time and space and who we think we are; finally, as we went through the third door, we would enter an exquisite stillness of peace and sacredness, there to receive guidance or healing or peace, whichever was most needed.

I had been trying to suppress what seemed to me an idle question, reflecting only curiosity and impatience, but I could not help asking Genesis about the baby. I made my question twofold: Was there anything he would like to say about the baby, and could he clear up another issue which had been causing me concern? Genesis responded only to the latter part of the question, which led us to speak about the purpose of life. "Can one ever rest?" I asked him. I was thinking of my sense of increased love and how satisfied I felt with that. "It seemed to me that it was worth attaining love. But I can't see beyond that."

"That is because there is nothing at this moment that you need to see as beyond that," he answered. "It is worth it to attain a clarity of love, yes, indeed. What else is there of value in the universe, in yours or in mine?"

"That is what it seems to me one would incarnate for," I answered, "to experience human love." I was thinking of the baby and what might have drawn it here. Who knows how many flavors of love there are in this universe? Perhaps, of all the varieties, this soul had chosen to experience that softened love which comes from loving what one knows is mortal, Shakespeare's "to love that well which thou must leave ere long." Is it not worth coming to earth to experience this love?

"Yes, it is," Genesis agreed. But his next statement was perplexing: "It is also why you disincarnate."

And Genesis went on, warming to his subject: "There is no difference in the love you seek in your universe or the abundance available in mine. It is one and the same universe. There is only one thing that separates you and me, and Michael and me, and Caroline and me. And it is simply a vibrational pattern, not anything else. We are creatures of the same universe, and we require forever to be in the presence of love."

This was heady stuff for me, in agreement with what was at my very core. Not only was Genesis speaking of love, but he was filling the room with it. I could feel the love vibrating in our atmosphere, and I wanted to rest in it. But maternal attachment was pricking at me, and I could not restrain myself. Smiling at the irrepressibility of a mother's concern, I repeated my earlier question—as if a being of Genesis' stature could possibly have forgotten: "Do you wish to speak about the baby?"

Genesis' last words to us were in answer to this question: "I wish to tell you to smile and know there are no accidents in the universe, and all is always perfectly timed."

The potency of his words would be proved as the pregnancy ran its course. How often those last words would echo in my mind.

Part Two

Like someone tracing the development of an artistic movement, I see the pregnancy divided into periods. First there was the Early Period, which involved some speculation, much concealment, and a simple, hopeful joy. Next came the Middle Period, in which I lost sight of you, my energy consumed in mere endurance. And finally there was the Late Period, all too brief.

The struggle of the Middle Period was so intense that it

occupied me totally. I now recognize your sure intention behind the difficulties. And I know that in truth, this stage of the pregnancy gave me more than the earlier one ever had. I was not growing from the innocent hopefulness of those early days; I was simply enjoying. Now I would have to grow.

Was it growth? Or was it just discovering that there was more in myself—more strength and more subtlety—than I had known, and did that discovery feel like growth? All I know is that in the midstage of this pregnancy, you were in eclipse. You put yourself in eclipse so that I could find my own strength. For all your many gifts, I thank you.

The Early Period raced swiftly to a close. It was on a Thursday, the last day of October, that the amniocentesis results were telephoned. What a relief! Now I could shed the veils of secrecy. But on Friday I told one teacher only. I thought that if I told my students, they might go home and stew all weekend, anxious over our future parting. I would wait until Monday, when we would have a chance to be together for five days in a row, and they could experience the fact that they were not really losing me, at least not for months.

On my way home from school, I decided to stop in a nearby town for a video to watch over the weekend. My use of home video was significant. For years I had lived with my head in the clouds or, more accurately, in the sands of antiquity. Ancient Greece, ancient India, the lands of the Biblical patriarchs—my mind was more often "there" than "here," no matter where "here" might be. The twentieth century just did not interest me. But with the teaching job came a plunge into modern times. Skateboards and brand names, boom boxes, and TV stars became part of my daily life.

At first it was a kind of willy-nilly thing; I was in no way prepared. Taking the teaching job was like jumping off a diving board into a lake, with fingers pinching my nostrils shut: "Ready or not, twentieth century, here I come." Gradually I began to embrace the change, to make it a matter of conscious decision. And stopping for a video was part of that. "If I've jumped into the waters of this century," I reasoned, "I might as well go for a swim." This would at least have the charm of novelty. And besides, it might serve my old aspirations toward perfection, which I had not quite given up. It seemed to me that all the saints of history achieved their state by being one hundred percent themselves; and embracing the century to which I had been born would be at least a start.

And so, after years of never watching television or listening to the radio and only rarely reading a newspsaper or going to a movie, I became a member of a video club. Watching movies at home with my family would be a pleasant way to join the mainstream.

Looking back, I see that most momentous events in my life have had their foreshadowing as well as their enormous aftermath. And so it was with the event which changed the pregnancy from a time of optimism to a time of learning and a testing, the event I call "disaster," though I can now see the gift, nestled like a pearl, within it. The disaster occurred at 3:00 Monday morning. But the whole weekend was a foreshadowing, starting with that Friday drive home from the video store.

I was unaccountably irritable on the way home. Normally

I am not a competitive driver. But that evening I was muttering to myself about any driver who cut me off or otherwise slowed me down; and every red light caused a small flare of anger. I was puzzled by this. I did not realize that I was entering the realm of estrangement, which would be my pattern for the weekend.

The weekend passed as a series of estrangements and what-if's, though I did not recognize the pattern until later. Each estrangement was seen in isolation, and the what-if's were events which seemed ordinary enough at the time, earning their title only later, in the light of the subsequent disaster. I know now that you never meant to spend a childhood with us. I know that you timed everything according to your own unfathomable wisdom. But still, even now, I cannot help letting those what-if's scurry through my mind like attic mice:

What if I had not eaten that dead, stale, way-too-minty canned chocolate cake, a "bargain" I had once bought on sale at the gourmet counter? (Bargain? Or did it cost a life? I know, dear one, you never meant to stay. But still, it would be months before I ate mint or chocolate again.) What if Michael and I had not made love? What if I had not taken a nice, long warm bath, or had not carried the heavy plastic vat I use for a tub?

Just like the real mice in our attic, once heard, these thoughts keep up their patter. What if I had gotten enough sleep, and not stayed up late Friday and Sunday night? What if I had not worn that black dress? And the strongest what-if of all, the one that stays riveted in my memory so that I can bring myself precisely back to the strain and breathless-ness of it: what if I had not given in to a fit of coughing?

On Saturday morning the family was having breakfast to-gether, and I was eating grapefruit. Joshua, who has his fa-ther's fine sense of humor, made an outrageously funny re-mark.

As I laughed at his joke, a shred of grapefruit must have gotten caught in my windpipe, for I began to cough and choke. I could witness the whole process. After years of summer allergy, I have grown used to watching myself de-cide when and how long to let myself cough.

"This coughing will be abrupt and uncomfortable for all. Maybe I should stifle it, drink some water, and cough more gently. But it will take much longer that way, and I want to be done with it. Oh, why don't I just hurl myself to the winds, cough my head off, and finish quickly?" I did that. There was a hurricane of coughing, much worse than I ex-pected. And I remember asking at the end, my voice weak and wistful as a small but steady stream of breath returned:

"It felt as if I could cough the baby out. I couldn't do that, could I?"

What-if's and estrangement. We watched our video Saturday after breakfast. And then I sat at the dining room table with books spread about me, happily immersed in my reading on the Bushmen of South Africa. I am a concentrator; one of my greatest pleasures is to lose myself in concentration. And this morning I was feeling how this was one of the loveliest parts of teaching: that I could dip myself totally in reading on a subject I love, and then share the riches with my students.

But Elena had nothing to do, and she was sitting near me at the table approaching an explosion. I could feel her dissatisfaction with life this morning, as she contemplated the empty day ahead, and her mounting desire to have me as a companion who would take away that pain. Soon I would be asked to take on a mother's task: to relieve her boredom and take away her sourness by absorbing it myself.

"I don't want to play, I want to read," a voice inside me insisted. I could feel resistance and resentment start to grow, with self-pity coming to crown them. "Is it too much to ask for?" the voice inside began to whine. "All I want is to sit in my own house and read without disturbance." And before any request was made, before my poor daughter could even get a word in, I announced stormily that I could not stand the pressure, that I was leaving the room to work elsewhere, and that people should act as if I were not home.

I withdrew and concentrated on the Bushmen to my heart's content, forgetting about lunch and emerging five hours later at 4:00 in the afternoon. Michael and I discussed how to time the evening, for we had arranged to eat dinner at a restaurant. Should we leave soon and eat early, as Michael would prefer? Or should I take a bath, so I would be relaxed and feel my best for dinner? Michael was content with my choice to take the bath and went off to play football with the children.

On the way to the bath I passed the computer and realized I needed to do some typing. I had prepared letters for the staff and for my students' parents announcing my pregnancy. But the letters needed some revision, and I wanted to have them photocopied in town when we went to dinner. I stopped at the computer and revised the letters. Had it been an ordinary typewriter, I would have stopped, I swear it. But the video screen cast the usual hypnotic spell—familiar to its many victims—and I stayed on the computer doing other typing chores. Suddenly it was time to dress for dinner.

When I got Michael from the football game and told him I had been typing and had not taken a bath after all, he was bitterly disappointed. I could understand what he was feeling; it had been hard for him, with my intense school preparations taking their toll. He told me he had been getting only the crumbs of my company lately. "I give you my full company," he said. "Why can't you give me yours?" Tonight he had been hoping for real darshan, for some full and warm, one hundred percent human interaction with postbath me. But now, he said, instead of getting that, he would be getting just more crumbs, with post-computer me.

The final estrangement: from Michael, my partner of twenty years, the person who was my surest anchor to the full warmth of the human experience. Though we were feeling distant, the momentum of our plan was strong, and so we started on our drive to town. But as we drove, Michael's discontent mounted. We parked the car and talked, trying to ease our feelings and salvage an evening out, but we could not. Sadly we turned the car around and drove back home.

Without much appetite, Michael and I nibbled at some leftovers for dinner. I read aloud to the family for a while. And then—what a relief—the day was done.

On Sunday Michael and I did manage to correct our course. One day late, I took my warm bath and we went out for dinner. On the way we stopped at the library. Now that the amniocentesis results were in, I could let myself prepare wholeheartedly for the birth. I had gone through the births of both my children without anesthesia, and so home delivery seemed the next thing to consider. We approached the matter by loading up on books about pregnancy, nutrition, and delivery. Then we stopped to make copies of the letters of announcement, and went on to a restaurant for dinner.

I can remember two moments of that dinner perfectly. One was a moment of puzzlement. Once the amniocentesis results came, we thought we would tell everyone we knew about the pregnancy. But that night a friend came over to our table in the restaurant, and we did not tell her. Later we stopped at her table to talk some more, and still we did not reveal our secret. I kept wondering why. It seemed the logical thing to do, and yet there was a barrier. Perhaps it was awkward because we had waited so long to tell. Or perhaps we simply did not have the habit yet. But I cannot help wondering whether it was because we knew: At some subconscious level, we were keeping our lives simple by not telling news we would only have to untell later.

The other moment came as I sat alone at our table while Michael was in the washroom. I was wearing a black dress that night. We had lived in Jerusalem during an early year of our marriage, and I had bought this dress in the Arab market—a large, tentlike black dress, beautifully embroidered. Years later, after I awoke to God, I learned meditation with a group which wore only white. Drawn to their ways, I began to avoid dark colors, and soon developed an aversion to wearing black. And so the black dress stayed in the back of my closet, unworn for years.

This night I took it out. I remember a moment of superstition: "Will it bring bad fortune to wear black?" But I was getting big, and the black dress was the only one that fit my requirements: big enough for comfort, festive enough to match my dinner mood, and concealing enough to keep my secret, in case I met someone connected with my class.

Now, alone at the table, I saw my reflection in the window. There was the black dress, looking not at all unlucky, and there was a shining face, with a soft smile and a light in the eyes. I liked what I saw, and I was surprised by how much joy I saw in that face. It looked lovely to me—contented, hopeful, at peace. I heard a cheerful, lilting voice inside me: "I happy."

What a surprise! The pitch and timbre of the voice were mine, but the melody and wording belonged to Timmy, whom I knew from a nursing home where I had been a volunteer. Timmy was a chubby, childike person with a heart of sunshine, a retarded man loved by all. When we would have a sharing circle after meditation, Timmy would announce, with the greatest sincerity and the most satisfied smile: "I happy." And seeing him sitting in his wheelchair beaming, looking for all the world like a merry, spinning top, I would know his words were true.

Now, hearing Timmy's words in my mind, I sensed the reason. Had the words been mine, I would have suspected them. How many times have I fooled myself, claiming to be happy when I only wished or thought I was? But Timmy was incapable of deceit. And when I heard "I happy" with just his lilt, I knew that for once I was, like Timmy, truly and simply happy.

As I remember these moments now, another voice speaks in my mind, a voice that rarely comes, bitter and mocking, the opposite of Timmy's. "Fix that moment," it says, taunting me. "Fix it in formaldehyde. Pin its butterfly wings in the album of memory." The voice is telling me that the happiness is memory only, a feeling I will never have again. And for a long time the voice has been right. That trusting, easy optimism of the Early Period would never return, not for a single instant of the pregnancy.

We drove home from the restaurant. Michael went to sleep at our normal early hour, but I had school preparation to do. I stayed up until midnight. Before going to sleep, I checked everything one last time: The auspicious coconut was in the refrigerator for tomorrow's announcement of the pregnancy—at least as auspicious as the opening of school! The announcement letters to parents and staff were all prepared and stuffed in their envelopes. Tomorrow's lessons were all in order. And the books on pregnancy were neatly arranged on the bookshelves. Surveying my little realm like a monarch, I felt the utmost satisfaction: Everything in my kingdom was in order. Tomorrow, finally, I would tell my class the news.

*I*t is 3:00 in the morning. I wake up wet. The bed is wet. Could I have urinated in my sleep? Once, when I was twenty-two, I had a nervous dream about auditioning for a play and woke to find that I had wet the bed. Can that have happened one more time?

I am curious, a bit disoriented, but not yet scared. I get out of bed and go to the bathroom. Everything is wet. My nightgown is drenched. Can it really be bed-wetting? I remember passing by the beds of bed wetters at overnight camp; the beds would reek with the stench of old urine. But there is no urine smell here, none at all. I am sniffing like an animal. My mind may be racing, but its thoughts are overwhelmed by the tide of animal instincts that rise to the surface as I frantically sniff my bedclothes: There is almost a salty smell.

Salt water? Salt water—ocean, our native element, the element in which all unborn babies swim, carrying memories of those early beginnings. So say scientists. Salt water. Amniotic fluid? I remember from other pregnancies how, if the "bag of waters" breaks, the birth must follow within twenty-four hours to prevent infection. Salt water? Amniotic fluid? Am I about to deliver?

The thought sets off an alarm in me. I begin to breathe rapidly, audibly panting, and I cannot stop. Rapid breathing, the pneumatic "hnhh hnhh hnhh" of breath forcibly blown out and inhaled again.

This trips off another memory. I recognize the category which I call "time crunch": those incredible moments when events which made no impression at the time are retrieved from memory years later, seemingly out of the blue, their relevance suddenly unveiled.

Three years ago I had phoned my neighbor. She was breathing rapidly on the phone, just like this. She said, "I can't talk to you now. Can I phone you back?" Two years later she explained to me, "Remember that time you called and I couldn't talk to you? Well, I was having a miscarriage then."

Miscarriage? Her words had meant little to me. I had accepted them naively, as a child might, leaving my cardboard image of miscarriage intact. Somewhere inside me was the childish idea of miscarriage as something momentary and antiseptic: you went to the hospital to have a baby, but instead you had a miscarriage. Only now, at this moment, do I think further to what miscarriage really means, think to the blood and fluid and body of an unborn child.

Miscarriage? Am I having a miscarriage? Here I am, breathing hard. The sound of my breath carries me back to my neighbor's sound on the phone. And the evidence of salt water—the spilled salt water of my inner ocean—is all around me. Total animal fear sets in.

I go back to bed. I lie panting hard, with my legs up, hoping by any means possible to keep this baby in. I enlist gravity and blind hope in my aid.

I awaken Michael. He calls the doctor, with the expected response: There is nothing we can do, wait until morning, when the medical center is open.

I begin to have weak contractions, five minutes apart. They last about half an hour.

Then I have a bout of pure crying. This crying is beyond thought and almost beyond sorrow. It is a kind of impersonal crying that takes me over. It is pure sorrow. Sorrow at the withdrawl of life. Whatever it was in me that once greeted the news of pregnancy with joy is now emitting a howl of pure despair.

I can feel the life ebbing out of me. My reaction is a totally thoughtless, almost feelingless pitch of sorrow. Then all ceases. I lie awake for hours without thought, then sleep briefly.

I come half awake and muse on those hours when I was neither awake nor asleep, neither conscious nor unconscious. What was really happening?

At the level of the body, surely there was some burst of hormone that had brought the crying in its wake. And at the level of the mind, there was simply zero—a state I have learned to appreciate through meditation, no matter how it comes. (And has not despair, my old friend, always been my surest path to thoughtlessness?) But beyond body and beyond mind, there was yet something else. What?

At the level of the soul, there was an anguish that was both intense and distilled of all impurities. For hours my very being had been one single wail.

I reach a state of further wakefulness and by habit put my hand to my belly to feel its reassuring curve. My belly is flat! (How did I not notice before?) The realization comes as one last pure wail.

That belly, that wonderfully round Madonna's belly, now flat! I am in mourning for that belly. And will a baby be able to survive this loss?

Yet throughout the night I have felt the baby kicking strongly, and there is still kicking now. Can a baby live through this?

As soon as the children were packed off to school and it was a suitable hour, we drove to the medical center. I rode in the back seat of the car lying down. I had hardly left my lying-down position since discovering the leak. As I got into the car, I was all right. But somewhere en route my mind drifted to pictures of two earlier trips to the hospital, happy and excited ones, to have a baby. I feared this trip was to discover that the baby was dead or dying, and the reversal tore me apart. I cried the rest of the way in.

Dr. Baker examined me and said that from what I described, it certainly sounded like a rupture of the amniotic sac, but he could not "prove" it. Could not *prove* it! In my mind I heard a shriek of recognition. It would be funny if it were not so serious. My meditation teacher had once commented on how people are not aware of their inner truths. "You are like people who, if their house is on fire, don't believe it until they read it in the newspapers." This had always seemed an odd statement to me, and I pondered it for years. Gradually I began to see that he was right. How often do people find out that they have ulcers and then realize they have been feeling a lot of tension? How often do I walk to the thermometer on a winter day to see if I am "really" cold, or notice that I have made a hurtful remark only when I can see the effects on another? But this one was the ultimate. "What!" I was thinking. "My wonderful Madonna belly is flat, the waters of my salt ocean have leaked all over my bed and bedclothes, and this doctor can't *prove* a rupture?"

Dr. Baker's manner was compassionate, and my tears were streaming the entire time. He tried to be reassuring, saying that since he could not prove a rupture, we should just hope for the best. Of course I should go home and get plenty of rest. In fact, he said, I might have to stay in bed until the birth of the baby. If it was a rupture, that would be the only therapy possible. But, he added, a rupture at twenty weeks was early; and if this was a rupture, he doubted I could carry the baby long enough.

I went home and lay in bed as long as I could. Then I lay down on the floor next to the wood stove in our dining room. Finally I could not stand being horizontal one second more. I reached for some pillows and arranged a position where, though my legs were stretched out on the floor, at least I could sit up and read. Fortunately, I had some more Bushman reading to do for class. And so I tried to forget myself and tune into this group of beautiful people and their stories. But a Bushman story "woke" me with a shock from my attempt at oblivion.

I was reading a chapter about hunting and came to a legend where the Bushman hero-hunter pierces the amniotic sac of a pregnant elephant and all the fluid rushes out. I was jolted back to full awareness of my condition. How could this be? Not once in my whole life, except when intentionally reading about pregnancy, had I ever come near a reference to the outpouring of amniotic fluid. How was it possible that today, of all days, I had read this passage? There was no avoiding it: this was a clear signature. I could see the master planning behind it all.

I can remember the sourness, the pessimism, of that moment perfectly. The whole of the timing came to me, all the pieces of the puzzle rearranging themselves to fit into a whole. That the conception was impossible I had long known. But now I saw the rest: Was it not curious that I discovered I was pregnant one day after I first began to feel I could last the year teaching? And how was it that so few people knew about the pregnancy? I, who am normally so communicative, could count the people who knew on my fingers: three friends whom we intentionally told, and one more friend to whom we blurted out the news because he happened to phone at the right moment, plus four at work. Even my parents did not know yet, nor my sister.

Later Michael would add another refinement. Not only did we keep the pregnancy remarkably secret from others, but also from ourselves. We had counted on it for a surprisingly short time. Except for that wonderful visit with Caroline, there were only three days on which we had let ourselves fully expect a healthy child. So: a pregnancy which we counted on for three days and which eight people knew about.

How was it that the leak had happened when I was at the absolute pitch of readiness to tell—with the coconut ready, the words of announcement prepared in my mind, and the letters of announcement stuffed in their envelopes? And finally, now there was this impossible coincidence of the Bushman legend of the amniotic fluid. Clearly the happy birth I had been hoping for was never meant to be.

If a soul was planning on a disappearing act, we must see that it was being remarkably gentle with our feelings. Yes, dear one, in retrospect I can see how well you orchestrated all of this. You gave us all you could, and in light of what you had in store for us, you shielded us as much as possible from pain. No wonder Genesis had avoided the question about the baby at first. He knew, didn't he? And through it all, I could hear his words repeating in my mind: "Smile and know that there are no coincidences, and all is always perfectly timed."

On Tuesday I went back to the medical center and saw another doctor. The leaking had subsided and my belly was swelling out again. The baby was still kicking, and so there seemed to be some grounds for hope. Dr. Entemann did a simple salt test, saw the salt crystals feathering under the microscope, and confirmed the rupture. He told me that the chances of successfully carrying the baby were extremely poor. He was not convinced real sealing ever occurred. Bed rest was the only suggested therapy, but he was not convinced that bed rest ever worked. Yes, in rare cases people carried a baby to term. But no one knew why; and my rupture was unfortunately early. The danger was that I would become infected and, as a measure of self-protection, would deliver the baby at once. And if I became infected and did not deliver, they might have to deliver the baby early in order to save my life.

There was a difficult decision now. Should I quit my job—— or take a long leave of absence, which felt the same to me— in order to stay in bed on the chance of bringing this baby to term? How could I? I am a restless and energetic person. Just one day of lying down had made me want to scream. And this job had been so terribly important to me. For three years it had been the focus of my attempt to grow out of an old and suffocating way of life. Was I really ready to sacrifice it? And, trickiest of all, *did* we really want this baby? Yes, we had been delighted. But it was the delight, for me at least, of unsought treasure, the delight of life choosing us.

The charm of the baby had been in its choice of us. But now that charm was gone. It seemed that *we* must choose the baby. For me to stop working and stay in bed would be to act out of strong desire. But that strong desire was not there, never had been. I did not want a baby: I wanted a being who wanted me.

The doctor said he did not recommend bed rest, and I did not want it, either. I planned to continue teaching, but in all other respects live my life as horizontally as possible. When I voiced this thought as I was leaving, I could see the nurse look at me as if I were a murderess. But what impressed me most was my reaction—or rather, lack of reaction—to what I saw as I walked out through the waiting room.

This was an obstetrics-gynecology clinic, and there were

women in the waiting room, some pregnant and others having come for a postpartum checkup. Many had brought their children or their newborn babies with them. Seeing the pregnant women, I realized that although I had loved the feel of my own rounded belly, I had not been drawn as usual to the look of pregnant women. And when I looked at the new babies or young children, my heart did not go out at all to them. How strange that I, who was crying over the loss of my baby, did not feel drawn to any baby or child I saw.

My mood all Tuesday was ominous. "Leaking" was the word which summarized it all. There was a leak of life in me, a leak of strength, a leak of hope. I was so exhausted from it all. It seemed the lying down itself was exhausting me. Or was I exhausted from my body's trying to replenish lost fluid? Or was I losing too much salt? Deficient in iron? There were still some powerful hormone releases. Any sad story could set me off into a freewheeling sense of universal loss. Leaking. Leaking, all the time.

I went to sleep early Tuesday night in a mood of depression and despair. I fell into a deep and satisfying sleep. Michael told me later that I talked in my sleep, unintelligibly—something I never do. Could I have been getting guidance as I slept?

I woke Wednesday feeling strong and optimistic. "Why have I been so defeated, so passive?" I asked myself. "I can heal this rupture. The doctor said there *are* some rare cases of a safe delivery. Well, why should I not be one of these? I am strong, I am capable, I am determined." I saw that I had been wallowing in despair, waiting for the inevitable end. Now I would try to *do* something. This was the way of the warrior.

I sat to meditate and spent the whole time with visualizations that would bring strength and healing. I began with the image of green—just fields of green imagined in my vision, the green of strength, the green of healing. Then I knit a green mesh bag for the baby to lie in. It was like a little green hammock, but gathered at the top, hanging down like an oriole's nest. Green only? No, it needed some gold, the gold light of love and healing. Like an oriole adding fancy threads to its nest, I wove in some golden threads. Carefully and patiently, one by one I added in those threads.

But this was only love and security for the baby. What about the physical healing itself? After all, my tissues were damaged, and that is why the fluid was leaking out. I changed images and pictured the healing taking place. I remembered a particularly ecstatic look at a piece of freshly cut apple under the microscope. The drops of apple moisture were glistening like the clearest crystal, and I was entranced. What I saw under the microscope gave me a sense of the crystalline arrangement of the apple cells, each one nestled within the carefully angled network of its neighboring cells as in a beehive, each glistening with its own juice. So now I pictured the cell tissue of my womb. The cells were glistening, and across a dangerous gap, from either side, the crystalline structure was growing, patiently adding to itself, reaching from side to side, one glistening cell after another, to bridge the gap and close off that ominous leak.

I played with images like a master architect. I could have

been an old Belgian woman dressed in black, carefully tatting my delicate lace, or a young child with an erector set.

When I was finished, I got up with resolve and showered. Should I not do the laundry, too? Yes, wash all the old clothes, tainted with fear and the leak of salty water, to put a border on the past.

I now saw all this as a test of the baby. If it was meant to be—if the baby was a strong soul, strongly wanting me— this would prove it. With the care and attention I would give it, any soul could preserve its physical life—*if* it so desired.

The days of the week went by. Diane, my principal, was also a registered nurse, wise in the ways of mishaps such as these. She had told me to take the entire week off, living close to my normal life. If I were going to deliver early, which was what she expected, it would probably happen before the week was out. There was a school holiday, Veteran's Day, the next Monday. And so altogether I would have eight days to be at home, adjusting to my new situation.

My feelings during the week varied. I barely thought

about class, my attention was so centered on the baby. Of course I could not hold to optimism full time. But on the whole I *did* adopt the warrior's attitude: I was determined and firm in my refusal to picture the worst. It was not until the eighth day, though, that I reached a balance, an attitude which I could wholly embrace.

The shift came during a meditation early Monday morning, on Veteran's Day, my last day at home.

I am trying to surrender, to bow to the grand pageant of life with all its actualities and possibilities, including my fear and pain, including the baby's life and the baby's death.

I cannot quite do it. Although I want to be able to accept all, when I sense my heart's desire, I find myself able to ask only for the baby's health and a "successful" birth.

"I cannot find a request that is not selfish," I apologize inwardly. "How can I simply surrender fully to what is?"

A voice answers me. A voice! It has been so long. I have at times heard these voices, mostly during meditation, instructing or comforting, and sometimes joking. These voices mean much to me. For they keep me from feeling adrift in the universe and anchor me to my own inner truth. But I have not the ability to summon them at will, and I have been waiting so long to hear one.

The voice speaks to me: "Don't you see, you don't need to do any act of surrender now. Your very being is surrender." Ah, it is the voice of the Comforter, the voice that warms me most.

I understand. He is saying that beneath it all, I have been surrendered all along. Yes, I can almost see that.

Tears fill my eyes. The voice is dim and distant, without its usual vibrance. But it is the Comforter.

"How can I reach you?" I ask. "And why has it been so long?"

"You have only to go down the corridor to hear me in my fullness." The voice is growing more vibrant, though still heard as if from afar.

The answer clearly refers to the exercise given by Genesis. I remember his instructions: to go through three doors, taking ten paces for each, leaving behind the physical at the first door, the mental at the second, and at the third door crossing to guidance, healing, or peace.

I cast about for imagery, to construct my corridor and doors. I begin in a sort of cathedral.

I picture blue mosaic tiles. I can see various shades of blue, with gold shining forth in places. Another time crunch! I am awed. I remember stopping at a fabric store in New York City fifteen years earlier. There was some imported silk from Italy, a beautiful mosaic pattern of blues and gold. It was expensive, and I asked for a snip of material to mull over a purchase. For years I kept that snip in a "nostalgia" file without knowing why. Now I knew. I had somehow recognized my inner sanctuary without even knowing that it existed.

Vivid shades of blue and the gleam of gold. The light of candles or oil lamps—many of them—flickering in niches in the side walls. Can this be a Byzantine church we visited in Jerusalem?

I go on constructing my space. What can I use for a floor? I remember the stone floor belonging to the Via Dolorosa in Jerusalem. I actually stepped on those stones, where Jesus had walked—my first experience of the holy. Then I had no name for what I felt. Only later, when God came to life for me and I grew familiar with the holy, could I go back and recognize those moments as the first.

It is not so much that the floor of my space is made of those lovely, massive, square-cut stones. But they give the feeling. A sort of luminous gray.

I see a corridor going off to one side and follow it.

The door at the end gleams white. Stucco, like the walls of the corridor, but shining brighter. Arched, with curved and polished wood all round. A heavy door.

I take ten steps towards the door, one step with every breath. I heave myself against the door. And leave physicality.

I haven't really left the physical realm, have I? But I do feel different. It is as if I really had a body moments before, and now I am left with only ideas about my body. Yes, I can still feel my knee if I try. But that's fair enough. After all, I haven't lost my mind yet. And what is the feeling in my knee right now except an idea in the mind?

I walk. I take the next ten steps. I am at the second door. This door is not as massive, and its light is different. It is moonlike in its quality, not a bright white moon but a dimmer sort.

How shall I go through this door? It would be inappropriate to heave myself against it. I haven't any body to heave with! How then shall I open it?

I do not open the door. I go through it, by mental decision.

I am a point now. This is really curious. I don't feel I have left ideas behind or that I have gone through a door, really. And yet there is this clear sense of being a point.

I advance as a point, sort of "beaming" a line out of myself as I go. The teacher in me is amused: Geometry is real—all that business about lines and points!

I am at the third door now.

I simply go through. I translate through. There is no effort, and no decision. It is a happening. One moment I am a point before a door. The next moment there is only the door. And the moment after that, the door is left behind. Only "I" am not there to be aware of the door behind me.

There is only light, and I am in the light. It is not one of those grand "I've seen the light" experiences. There are no feelings whatever, and no knowing.

I am not the source of the light. But I am in the light. But I am not a point in the light or anything—any thing—in it.

Ideas return. What will I teach tomorrow? And so on. But I want to stay longer in the light. I must.

I decide to retrace my path. I return to the corridor and quickly go through the three doors one more time.

After a while I feel the pull to leave again. I examine it this time. What is it exactly that is pulling me away? Is it my body—a pain in the knees, a strain in the back? No. I scan and feel that my body is "empty." This is precisely how I have been feeling about the baby: the empty chair. Well, why could it not be that way for me, too? At this moment my consciousness is totally withdrawn from my body.

Then what is pulling me? Is it my mind? Some thoughts? I scan my mind. I enter the mind realm. Now this is strange, this is a revelation! How did I never notice this before? My mind is thinking, but "I" am not really in it, any more than I am in my body. My mind, too, is an empty chair.

I try to understand this, but it is hard. I notice the tendency to assume I am in my mind, that if thoughts are

*there, then I must be there too, thinking them. But surely
there is enough input by now for thoughts to circulate on
their own. If computers can do it, why not my mind?*

What is pulling me back then?

*The point. Could that be pulling me back? It must be so.
But could I ever learn to dissociate from that point? Isn't
that point my very soul, the point-source of my being? To
learn to withdraw from my body and my mind is one thing.
But from my soul? Ah, that would be a trick!*

*It seems an impossibility. But this one time I must leave
that point behind. I want to be in that light. No, "in" is not
quite right. I was neither in the light, nor was I aware that
I was the light. Whatever it was, I must return one more
time. And there is a return.*

Yes. Light. Yes.

*And in this realm of light, an inward prayer is made:
"Whatever healing—if healing is needed—let it be. If there
is a rip in my soul which needs healing, strengthening, let
this be it. And if not, then let light just be around me."*

I had come into balance.

When I came out of the meditation, I sensed that what had
happened was significant: I had finally entered into the fullness of surrender. This was a true surrender. I was no longer
fearful of the baby's death nor anxious for the baby's birth.
If my physical body needed healing, let it heal. If this rupture represented a rip in my soul, let that heal. My soul
could heal with or without a successful birth. Only let it all
be for the light and in the light. I was now able to accept all.

It was six o'clock in the morning. Rather than lie down

again in bed, I forced myself to go downstairs and write down the whole experience in my journal. For such experiences are subtle and can vanish like a dream.

As I wrote, I gave Diane a breath of thanks for her advice to stay home all week and give myself time. I saw that I had needed every one of the eight days to work through the process of my inner change. And I needed the time also simply to rest, to gather strength needed for the shift. With the drain of teaching, I had let my meditations become irregular and lacking in force. Yet it was only here, in meditation, that I could find a true compass setting for my life.

Looking back, I could see the evolution of the past week: from despair to resolution to surrender. But not a weak surrender: a surrender with strength. I would do everything I could for this baby (short of lying on my back for ever more until delivery). But I would do it without desire. A difficult balance to achieve.

Writing in my journal, I made myself this promise: "I will say yes, welcome the life. I will be unwavering in my allegiance to this new life—but without desire."

I returned to school the next day. There was a sweet reunion, with a lot of love flowing. The girls spontaneously gathered and made me a "Welcome Back" book, with testimonies and signatures. And Arnold had bought a box of chocolates for me. I felt connected with my students, and warmed by their welcome. I was glad that I had not withdrawn from schoolteaching in order to pursue what was now looking like a phantom hope.

We sat in a circle and I gave them a chance to talk first.

They unburdened themselves about their suffering at the hands of a succession of substitute teachers.

Much later, in June, when we had our final circle, telling what we would remember most about this year, several students said it was the substitute teachers. This surprised me at the time and made me wonder: Had I made so weak an impression that the substitutes would be their most vivid memory? But when I reflected, I realized that it might mean quite the opposite: that they had come so to count on the friendship and comparative freedom I brought to our classroom that any loss was traumatic.

After the students had given me their news, I gave them mine. I had full range of choice as to how to do this. No one had even told them I was pregnant, and I could have gone on with my concealment. But I chose openness. This has always been my way, and the long concealment had been strain enough.

I let them see that I was deeply affected by my difficult situation, but I was careful not to let any pessimism or unhappiness come through. I explained my situation quite frankly, telling them the sequence of events, and I passed around some mysterious photographs, taken *in utero*, of a fetus about the age of mine. I explained to them what the problem was and what were the possibilities. All along I monitored their reactions. Had I sensed any fear or repulsion, I would have stopped. But what I saw was sympathetic interest.

The principal, however, told me the next day that one of the students had gone home upset by my news. She cautioned me that this was a first exposure to pregnancy for many of my students, and I should be careful that it not be a negative one. In retrospect I do not know if there was a better way to share the news. The openness was part of what was special in our classroom. And twenty years from now, what the students will carry with them of value may be just this: the memory of someone who did not shy away from difficulties and did not hide them.

I communicated openly with my class partly because that is my nature and comes most easily to me. But there was another motive as well: I had to enlist their aid. I felt that the baby was in danger and that the amount of motion I expended, with its correlate in leaking, might have an effect on the life or death of the baby. I needed to teach now in the most fluid-conserving way, which meant with the minimum of strain and motion. I would need to stay seated rather than stand, stand rather than walk. If my class would go downstairs to the cafeteria quietly, for example, I would not need to escort them down for lunch. And that would save me precious fluid. But how could I ask them to be extra quiet and well-behaved—every teacher's constant request—without letting them know the special reason?

What followed at school was a bleak period, a "calculus of leaks." The calculations had begun earlier, during my week at home. But life was simpler then, with fewer decisions. Now I had to deliberate on virtually every act.

I had done an experiment at home to find out how much fluid I was actually losing. Michael, a research scientist, marveled as he watched me: "I always knew you were the scientist of our family!" And I remember thinking, as I adjusted the weights on the scale, "If only science class could see me now! *This* is real science." I felt proud as any schoolchild with my little experiment—if only the purpose had not been so grim.

Carefully I had saved the absorbent pads I used over a

period of twenty-four hours, sealing them tightly in a plastic bag to prevent evaporation. I then took an equal number of dry pads and sealed them in the same manner. I weighed the bags against each other in the pans of a balance scale, adding metric weights on the dry side until the two sides balanced. Then I removed the pads and determined how much water was needed to balance those weights. In this way I found out that I was leaking about one-half cup of fluid every day.

One-half cup? That was not very much. Surely I could replace that. I would drink as much as possible. One-half cup. It seemed so odd to me. It would take just a few seconds to pour out half a cup of liquid; but while that small amount was being lost, I could feel the leaking—and the fear—full time.

And so I had to calculate. Driving our car took extra fluid from me because we had a stick shift. (Changing gears put extra strain on my pelvic muscles.) Ah, that decision made years ago when we bought our car was now costing me drops of precious amniotic fluid. And the trip I took to the homeopathic doctor's office: was it worth it? I had phoned a midwife and explained my condition. She had given me little hope, but she had named an herbal tea that might help. Like a pilgrim going to Lourdes, I carried my leaking body through the streets of a distant town, trying to get the herbal extract from the only doctor who had it in stock. Would it work? Would it save more fluid than it lost?

Once I was back teaching, my calculations increased radically. I had to be constantly alert. There was hardly a moment which did not call for a decision. And each decision, it seemed to me, affected probability: Would the baby live or die?

Immediately upon arrival I was faced with a decision: How many trips to carry in my two heavy bags? I could carry none, and wait for a student to arrive and help me. But no, I needed what was in the bags to set up my classroom. Two trips then? That would double my walking but lighten my load. Or all in one trip? That would be more strain, but over less time. Impatient by nature, and not knowing which was better, I carried in both bags at once.

It would be impossible, and painful, to give a true idea of the constant monitoring. One event stands out to summarize the whole: I was outside for recess duty and in the distance I could see a fight about to start. Whether to stop it or not? I reasoned it out: "If I shout, that will make me cough; and coughing will make me lose extra fluid. But if I don't shout, I will be failing to do my job." How can one weigh a life—or was it only the illusory hope of a life?—against *dharma*, the right-now demands of duty? I watched the developing fracas with an eagle eye. Finally, when I saw that the hitting was inevitable and the last moment at hand, I shouted out for the instigator to stop and come over to me. Sure enough, the effort made me cough. And the cough made more fluid leak out of me. But I had done my job.

So many little difficulties, and so many moments. Who could remember them all? (And who would want to?) My pitiful little "kit," with emergency dry clothes, absorbent pads, and plastic bags, that I had to take with me whenever I went to the bathroom. The many times I had to disappear, suddenly and silently, from the classroom for a bathroom trip, unobtrusively taking my kit from a desk drawer, hoping against hope that the students would not notice and would remain quietly at work. And the moment when a student entered the classroom and sniffed, remarking innocently, "It smells like a doctor's office."

I treated myself with extra care on the physical level. I ate only the most wholesome foods. No white flour at all, no caffeine drinks, and no more sugar snacks. I could have bought the cafeteria salads, for they were healthy enough. But the two cooks would glare at me as they dished salad onto my plate, hostile because I had once asked them to stop running the dishwasher during the students' lunch, and complained when they refused.

I did not understand then that they ran the machine while a hundred students were eating lunch, (increasing the cafeteria's already hellish din almost past endurance) so that they could have their own lunch afterwards in peace and quiet. I did not know that this was their only compensation for a grossly underpaid job. Still, even had I understood, theirs was a way of distorted calculation to which I could not agree. By their reckoning, the pleasure of two outweighed the pain of a hundred—as long as *they* were the two. I did not want my food to absorb their hostility, so I packed my own lunch every morning, although this had its cost in fluid.

On the days when I was lucky enough to escape the torture of cafeteria duty, I would eat my food in the peace of my empty classroom, while my students were at lunch. On many days these fifteen minutes would be the only stretch of quiet I would have; so crowded was our teaching schedule.

One moment stands out from this period of bleakness. I was sitting at the reading table at the back of my classroom, having lunch. I had started eating my healthy sandwich and went to pour myself some herbal tea. The thermos cap was on too tight. I could open it, but that would strain me and cause more leaking. And so I could not open it. I experienced a new level of helplessness. A fellow teacher was walking by and stopped to wave hello. "Linda," I called out, "could you open this thermos for me?"

It was so hard for me to ask for help. As Linda was opening the thermos, I reflected on how much courage and grace it must take to live with a permanent disability. My own, I knew, was temporary. Though in memory this period at school would feel like years of exile in Siberia, in fact it lasted all too short a time.

Only now do I appreciate the qualities and strength all this took. At the time, I did not allow myself to see how difficult it was. Perhaps that would have made me crumble. This was a period of training. And not seeing the difficulties was what allowed the training to take place. There was training in endurance—-the endurance of pain, fear, and fatigue. And there was also an exercise of will—the constant vigilance, the constant calculation, and, subtlest of all, the constant guarding of my attitude.

The first level of guarding my attitude was simply walling off the sense of difficulty, which was done without any conscious effort—a common human response. But also I had to keep myself from hopelessness or despair. I was constantly aware of my rate of leaking, and whenever I felt the rate accelerate, an inner alarm would sound. There was no way I could remain neutral in such a situation, but I permitted myself only a general sort of alarm. By my own rules, I was not allowed to cling to the fear or magnify it by linking it with any statement such as, "The baby will die." And finally, most delicate of all, I had to keep myself from feeling desire or hope.

I wanted to keep that balance I had bid for in my Monday morning meditation: the balance between surrender and determination. If I was not allowed, by my own rules, to fear the baby's death, no more was I allowed to hope for the baby's life. For if fear would keep me from determination, hope would keep me from surrender. But how could I continue to support the life of the baby without feeling hope or desire? I found for myself an attitude which seemed to strike the exact balance: allegiance.

I had used the word "allegiance" in my promise to myself after the Monday meditation. And all week long I got to see how well the word suited me. It amused me: Like so many others, as a schoolchild I had mouthed the word "allegiance" every day, mechanically, without any sense of meaning. But now, as I led my students in the pledge to the flag—my students, who were undoubtedly feeling the whole thing as mechanically as I had—the word "allegiance" began to resonate, came vividly to life.

We had discussed the meaning of the pledge of allegiance in class once. And I had told my students that while I could sincerely pledge allegiance to a country, I could not pledge allegiance to a symbol or a piece of cloth. To keep some shred of honesty, I would always lead off loudly, "I pledge allegiance . . ." then trail off into silence, resuming with ". . . to the United States of America." I always wondered whether my students would notice, but they never did.

All year I used this omission as a test of my being focused on the present moment, an established spiritual practice. If I ever heard my voice boom out "to the flag," which it occasionally did, I would know that I had lost my train of awareness—"spaced out" in the idiom of our rocket age. But these mornings, during the time of testing, I could not possibly space out. For I would be savoring the term "allegiance," mulling it over and feeling how well it suited me. "Yes," I would think, "I *do* pledge allegiance. I pledge allegiance to this life within me." I knew that I would offer myself to support this life without hoping or despairing, without a thought of the result. My job was simply to give myself over to maintaining life: and that was allegiance.

I got to see the truth of my own allegiance, the balanced quality of my commitment, one day when I stayed after school to talk with the principal. It was Thursday of that first week back at school, and our topic was my second social studies class, the one I had taken in trade with a neighboring teacher, so that he could have my students for science. That arrangment was a mistake. I had his students a total of two and a half hours a week, which was not time enough for them to grow accustomed to my ways. And I could not bring myself to adapt to theirs.

Although I tried to be charitable and to find qualities to admire in these students, I could not help thinking of them as my "class of sheep." I had once read of an experiment where sheep got so accustomed to running their mazes, grew so to "like" it, that they would run the mazes for no reward at all, even leaving behind their baby lambs, bleating pitifully for milk. These students were like those sheep. They were anxious to run the mazes of assignments and tests, and ill at ease with me because I did not place importance on their accustomed mazes. As for the lambs they left behind, these were their own precious sparks of freedom and inquiry. No matter how I tried to reach them, raising interesting questions or making provocative remarks, all I ever got was a dead look at best, mischief and noisemaking at worst, and occasionally that question which freezes the heart of all true teachers: "Do we have to know this for the test?"

Diane was as interested as I in the challenge of how to reach these students, and we batted around some ideas that day, as we had often done. As I turned to leave, she asked me how I was feeling about the baby. Seeing the extraordinary hardship I was going through, she assumed that I must want this baby terribly.

I tried to tell her of my balance: that I would do everything in my power to support the life of this baby, but without wishing or wanting anything. About to leave, hand on the doorknob, I said that I had learned my lesson. "I've been burned too many times by getting what I want." When Diane asked what I meant, I came back in to tell the story of the oriole.

Several years ago I had heard and seen an oriole for the first time. How glorious: the song as bright and orange as the body. I was entranced, and prayed that I would have many more chances to see an oriole. The universe listened and answered with a lesson. A female oriole fell in love with her reflection in the large window-door of my house. She would hurl herself repeatedly against the window with a series of sickening thuds, her mate sitting in the nearby bush, as if patiently waiting for her madness to end.

I feared that I had somehow caused this with my prayer, and I hoped the oriole would come to her senses before she was too battered to go off with her mate and make more orioles. And so the universe had granted me my lesson: Be careful what you ask for; it may be given you.

"I've learned that lesson," I told Diane. "I say yes fully to this life within me, but without desire."

How often do we come to know ourselves by seeing what we say or do with others? After that Monday morning's meditation I had hoped I was in balance, but could not be sure. Now, hearing how spontaneously I spoke those words, with no posing and no thought beforehand, I knew that the balance was no fiction: I was truly living it.

I am impatient, dear one. I feel myself approaching the moments when you were present in your fullness, and I long to meet you there again. But I must take one last detour. There are two demands on me. There is the urgent pull I feel towards you, which is surely why I am writing this. But also, the tale itself makes its own demands, asking to be told in a complete way. And so one final introduction must be made, to a group I called "the parents."

These were the parents of the students in my second social

studies class. I would not have known them as a group were it not for the fact that I introduced their children to that other group, "the Buddhists," which aroused their opposition. Although I met many wonderful people from the town of Southborough, when I think of that town even now, my first reaction is to remember "the parents" and cringe. They were, to my eyes, as small as the Buddhists were large.

At first I was not aware of them as a group. I knew only that individual parents of students in my second social studies class were giving me difficulty. They would telephone me at a rate far greater than the parents of my own students, who had me for so many hours more, and challenge me in vaguely hostile ways. One even complained about the faintness of my purple ditto sheets—as if I did not use the same aged machine all the other teachers did.

Even when the message was neutral, there was usually an undercurrent of hostility. One vaguely hostile call was from Mrs. Braski, who asked me early in the year whether I knew her daughter was partially deaf. When I said I did not but that I would be glad to make adjustments, she fended me off, telling me I should in no way treat her daughter differently, she just wanted me to know. It was Mrs. Braski who would bring my social studies unit to a close.

Before school began, I had inspected the American history textbooks allotted to my social studies classes and discovered that they could be read by an adult in less than two hours and contained a minimum of information. I estimated that we could learn the history in about half a year. (I was wrong, it turned out. I had not realized how slowly information is absorbed when there is no background.) And so I cast about for other material that would be interesting.

I realized that the Dome of Peace, due to be inaugurated

in October, would make a perfect field trip for my social studies classes. (And in fact, many classes from other local schools, and one entire school, made visits there that autumn.) Knowing that my students would get far more value out of their visit if they had some understanding, I decided to place our field trip within the context of a unit on world religions, a worthwhile topic in any case.

Michael warned me that the unit would not be acceptable unless I started with Christianity, which made some sense, since it was familiar to the students. But I knew that this would give the impression subtly that Christianity was the norm from which all other religions deviated. And I did not want to show any bias one way or another. Besides, there wasn't really time. I needed to start with Buddhism for the sake of the field trip. After that I would go back to Hinduism and present the five major world religions in their historical order: Hinduism, Judaism, Buddhism, Christianity, and Islam.

I cleared the field trip with the superintendent, and the religion unit with the principal. Knowing that religion can be a controversial topic, Diane advised me to send a newsletter to the parents, stating my goals. My letter contained the statement, unexceptional to me, that no religion would be taught as the "right" one, but that all religions would be treated with an attitude of interest and respect. Looking back now, I can see how my impartial approach must have been like a red flag to some parents. It would have been threatening enough, I think, to present five world religions as equally worthy of respect. But even worse—as the parents would soon find out—I was presenting them as equally *alive*.

I had once read that early religious training is like a vaccination, exposing us to the dead or attenuated strain of our religion so that if later the real thing comes along—the living presence—we will be immune, our systems ready to resist. Having had moving experiences within the frameworks of many different religions, I did not intend to be party to giving any such vaccinations. My intent was for all the religions to be seen in their vitality—with stories, rituals, and music. It never occured to me that to some of these parents, presenting Buddhism or Hinduism in a live way was tantamount to bringing in a live polio virus to a class on disease.

There were signs of trouble all along. I remember the janitor suspiciously eyeing the drawings students in my class had made of Buddha under the Bo tree, asking me about my own religious practices and whether they were satanic (!). And when I first announced the visit to the Dome of Peace, one irate parent from the second social studies class had called the principal and harangued her for half an hour, insisting that if students were going to visit a Buddhist dome, they should take equal time for a field trip to a church.

I received inquiries about the field trip from parents of the second social studies class. And finally there was the visit from Mrs. Rostak, who stopped in after school to explain her beliefs and offer names of people who could come in to speak on Christianity. She told me she planned not to send her son to the Dome of Peace because, as she said, "Jesus would not be pleased to see him there."

For a moment there flashed in my mind's eye a vivid picture of Jesus wearing blinders. I saw that in order to please this blindered Jesus, Mrs. Rostak was willing to wear blinders herself and also put them on her son. "No," I wanted to tell her, "Jesus is strong and confident, able to accept all sincerely seeking under the umbrella of his truth." But I said nothing. I nodded sympathetically and thanked her for being so open and sharing her views.

Mrs. Rostak was one of the group of four families from the second social studies class who formed a coalition to oppose me. She was the most open by far, and kind in her own way. When I saw her at school later in the year, I observed almost a halo of purity around her. Her devotion gave her family a nimbus of piety and love to live within. If she was, in my opinion, mistaken about how to safeguard her faith, at least she had something worth safeguarding—which is more than I can say for Mrs. Braski, who would become the leader of the group.

At the time of the field trip, I knew Mrs. Braski only from her voice on the telephone. Soon I would see her at school— a short, fiery woman, whose small stature seemed suited to her inner nature. When I think of Mrs. Braski, the image comes of a fighting cock or a prizefighter—bantam weight, of course. I found her a small-time person, aggressive and ambitious, fighting her battles in any available arena, whether it be a town meeting or elementary school. Her main interest was to stake out ever more territory to feed her need for power, for which she would gladly pose as defender of the faith.

The field trip went beautifully. We visited early in October, on my first day at school after learning I was pregnant. The Dome of Peace was still shining with its post-inauguration splendor. Many Buddhist monks and nuns from all parts of the world were still there, having come for the inauguration. There were forty-nine students, two teachers, and two parent chaperons. In addition there was one mother from the second social studies class who surprised us all by darting out of the driveway in her car when the school bus passed her house and tailing us all the way to the Dome—another sign of trouble, had I been aware.

The Buddhists outdid themselves in hospitality. At my request many of the monks had worn their ceremonial robes for our visit. (Otherwise they would have been hard at work, shovels in hand, distinguishable from the rest of the crew only by working harder.) We were escorted around the Dome for the traditional three times, with the chanting and beating of the Buddhist drums. Then we went into the altar room, where the monks and nuns performed additional rituals. Clara, an American Buddhist nun with warm heart and shaven head, gave explanations and answered the students' many questions, including the inevitable ones about her hair.

With radiant smiles, several girls from the second social studies class presented apples to the Buddhists, for they had learned that the Buddhists lived only on alms. It was a moment of gold, the only one I can remember with the students of that class. Then we were invited downstairs for tea and a Japanese snack. The snack, which included seaweed crackers, turned out to be one of the students' strongest memories. Later, when we were gathering our impressions to compose a thank-you note, I found, interspersed among remarks on the beauty of the Dome and the fervor of the chanting, many comments such as, "Monks eat strange food."

All this was past history that Thursday when I stayed after school and told Diane the story of the oriole. Almost a month had gone by since the field trip and, as far as we both knew, parental opposition had flared and then completely subsided. Neither of us was aware of the storm that was brewing. That very evening Mrs. Braski would be busy on the telephone, assembling her group.

On Friday morning I went to school curiously euphoric. I had reason to be happy. It was Friday, for one. And also I was anticipating the first chance to have a relaxation with only those who truly wanted it. Laney Barnes, a classroom mother who often helped, had agreed to come in and take part of the class for another activity, so that the students could have a choice. I was curious. Some students truly loved relaxations and had many varieties of experience— from rocklike "sleep" to picturing all the scenes of love in their lives, Christmas mornings and other times, with tears running. Others complained bitterly that it was boring and nothing happened at all. I suspected that even some of the bored ones got more out of it than they knew, and I was curious to see what choices would be made.

I was met in the hallway by Diane, who said we needed to talk quickly. As we were standing there, a short, red-haired woman with a tough, unpleasant manner brushed past me in a determined way without a glance and virtually pushed Diane aside, demanding to meet with her at once. Diane said calmly that she would be available in a few minutes, and pointed to an empty room. Then she and I went into my classroom and closed the door so we could talk without disturbance.

The woman was Mrs. Braski, a vehement opponent of mine, it turned out, and known as a terror by many in the town. Diane had time to say only this much: Four parents of students from my second social studies class were descending in a group to demand the close of my religion unit. Laney Barnes, as chairman of the school committee, would be there for the discussion of the religion unit, at least as a witness. There was to be no relaxation this morning. (Without Laney I could not have followed my plan anyway.) And I should just conduct class in a perfectly normal way and not do anything further connected with world religions.

The euphoria with which I entered school remained all day, despite Diane's news. I sailed through the spelling test, the math, and so on. Eventually Diane and I found time to talk. She told me what had happened at the meeting. Together we decided to drop the religion unit. Her reasoning was that she wanted parent support in the spring, when she would be trying to get a much-needed extra teaching position, and she did not want to jeopardize relationships now in a struggle over the religion unit. She acknowledged that there was an issue of academic freedom here. But this did not seem to be the right time to take a stand on that issue, especially since I would be leaving soon to have the baby.

I was not bothered by losing the religion unit, aside from the loss of time in gathering material. We would wrap up the unit with an antiseptic film I had ordered, to be screened first by interested parents. (The film turned out to be just right, presenting five major world religions with equal dullness.) We would make a chart with a few "dead" facts. And that was it. There would be no test. And there would be no real understanding. Then on to American history.

But this was only the beginning of the losses. Diane continued: she wanted me to keep a low profile generally. This meant no more relaxations. Also there should be no more breath count. And finally, on no account should we ever sit in a circle on the floor. She reasoned that if I were to "lay low," the opposing parents would forget about me, and I could be rehired in spring. But I felt a puzzle underneath it all: If I were stripped of all that made me different, why bother rehiring me?

I could see the point about relaxations; they *were* very unusual. But the breath count was so short and innocent, a simple way to start the day with quiet togetherness. (Ah, but the parents of my second social studies class called it meditation.) As for the circle, I could not accept that loss. A circle expresses solidarity and also creates it. Diane said firmly, "You'll just have to accomplish what you accomplish by circle some other way." I recognized the impossibility at once. "No," I thought. "You're wrong. For some things there are no substitutes. You might as well tell me to accomplish what I accomplish by smiling some other way. Certain things we just can't do without. We need smiles and the sun's warmth, and we need circles, too." For the first time I questioned whether Diane was as perceptive, and as sincere, as I had thought. There was no point in protesting at the moment: I remained silent.

Strangely enough, that very day we had our best classroom discussion ever, and without a circle. I had assigned a difficult reading passage by a naturalist who was doing fieldwork in Costa Rica and who had kept a journal. He was taking a strenuous hike from the jungle to town and was resting when a vulture began to circle above him. He felt momentary fear when the shadow passed over him but also a curious elation. I asked the class whether they ever felt that kind of mixture of feelings—"strange but joyous," in his words. Rona raised her hand and said, "Yes. When I *wonder*." "What kind of wondering?" I asked. Rona considered for a minute, drawing up an experience from the deep well of her memory. "When I wonder," she said slowly, "whether there has to be a world."

This answer excited the class. Students went into their other wonderings—what God is really like, what if we did not exist, and so on. Someone wondered about dreams— whether they are real, how is it that sometimes you dream you are being choked and wake to find the cat on your neck. That got us into the whole realm of dreams, with students volunteering stories as they never had before. They all stayed quiet for each other's stories, responded, and went on to new themes. The discussion lasted an hour.

At some point I saw students signal each other not to remind me of the time, as if they were tricking me. But I was aware of the time, delighted to let them go on. When the discussion was over, the genuine interest of the students was confirmed: Four boys came up to me at once asking to go to the bathroom. They had all waited because they did not want to miss what anyone was saying! This was one of those magical events in teaching: it all seemed so luminously worthwhile.

I stopped in to talk with Diane before leaving school that day. She was adamant on all counts: I could not continue the unit on world religions with my own students, who seemed interested; I must teach the same social studies to both classes. And no, there was to be no more sitting in a circle. She sympathized, she said. She had taught a class years before, and they had ended each day with a circle on the floor. Not only would I have to swallow this, but also be discreet about the cause, ending circle, relaxation, and breath count as if it were my own choice and not a decision dictated from above. I was hurt and puzzled. I admired Diane and valued the appreciation she had shown for my teaching. I feared I must have slipped in her estimation. And I also wondered why she had allied herself with the opposition. "The parents" had come bent only upon ending the religion unit. But Diane was robbing my class of far more than they had ever dreamed. Why should the parents of the other class wind up taking circle away from mine?

I came home exhausted but still euphoric, still sailing through the day. Michael suspected I was denying my true feelings. I examined myself. No, I *did* feel fine, pleased with myself. I had passed my own tests. I had never acted thoughtlessly or rashly. If anything, I had simply miscalculated. But I had acted out of generosity: to share, with love.

Michael reminded me of what Genesis had told Caroline, that when people take risks, the angels are happy. Or, as

Genesis said, "Your taking risks keeps us in business." Leaving home to teach had been such a risk; and the religion unit had been a risk within that risk. And it is true that the angels were happy. Or at least you, dear one, were pleased.

That evening I began having some odd pain, as if a wall were wearing thin. When the baby kicked in a certain place, it hurt like a bruise. And when my daughter accidentally brushed me there, I felt a sudden sharp pain as if jabbed.

I woke that night and found the amniotic fluid tinged with blood. This was new, and alarming. Timings again. I could not help but notice the intertwining of pregnancy and job: The life of my class and the life of the baby were coming to a close together.

Part Three

On Saturday I reached a low point, the turning point, the nadir of the curve. My courage and optimism were gone, but I had not yet moved into a relationship with you. I had lost sight of you, lost sight even of my love; so preoccupied was I with the attempt to keep the baby alive, an attempt that seemed about to end in failure.

I felt paralyzed. We telephoned the doctor, who said, as usual, not to worry and to come in Monday, when the medical center was open. And so I sat all day, knees locked, whole body tense, trying not to move, lest the rate of leak change and I feel it. I sat at the dining room table glued to my seat, doing school work for hours, not moving. I even kept myself from going to the bathroom, lest I see any more of the alarmingly pink fluid. As my body was locked, so was my mind: I was unable to face what was or what would be.

Now the euphoria was gone. I was depressed about school. I reproached myself for being a fool over the religion unit. Here I had wanted to teach in public school so badly, and see what I had done. Why could I not just have had more common sense? Why have I always been such an incautious person? Why had I not followed Michael's advice and begun with Christianity?

Worst of all, I could feel the pregnancy withdrawing. It was subtle. I could not convince anyone else. But I could feel the pregnancy leaving me. I knew that ripe feeling that comes with pregnancy, that wonderful feeling of filling out one's skin just a little more fully, of being ripe to bursting. But now, subtly, there had been a change. I did not fill out my skin quite as well as I used to. My feet even fit in my shoes without a flicker of rebellion. And, for the first time, I was cold. One of the delights of pregnancy had always been for me the extra warmth given by the additional blood supply. I enjoyed knowing I would never feel cold no matter what the season. But now I was having my first moments of chill. And for the first time, the baby was hardly moving at all. I was afraid.

There was one strange ray of comfort through it all, though. In my Bushman reading I had come across the story of a woman who delivered a baby too early. She had gone alone into the bush to give birth, as was the custom, and when the baby died, minutes after delivery, she buried it herself and walked back to her village. Reading the book, I had felt sorry for her. But now I felt at one with her; and that was somehow easier. I felt a new kinship with all women who had lost children. There was some excitement in this, as if I were discovering that doors could open any time. I was losing a baby, but look: I was gaining sisters all over the world.

By midmorning Sunday I could stand it no longer. Leaking or not, I had to do something to distract myself. Michael and I went to a vegetable stand to buy some sacks of winter vegetables. And then we went to a restaurant for lunch. During the time we spent at the restaurant, I went through many absorbent pads, each stained a deeper color. There was an agonizing sense of the end coming. It was speeding towards us, and yet so slowly. There was an underwater quality to it all, as if we were in a constant state of slow-motion emergency.

Michael and I sat across from each other and had a deep and serious talk. And now, dear one, you began to return. I had been preoccupied with the need for strength and endurance. But now, as that need began to wane, I came back into a relationship with you.

The extra love you had poured around me before went mainly to my class. But now Michael was held strong in that love. I remember sitting across from him at the table and being flooded by your grace. I was living the words of Sappho's poem, sung in the days when armies and navies stirred the heart: *Oi men hippeon stroton, oi de pesdon* . . . "Some say a troop of cavalry, some say footsoldiers, and some say a fleet of ships is the fairest sight on this black earth. But I say: it's the one you love."

I had learned these words in college many years before.

Like seeds they had remained dormant, but were sprouting now inside me. Looking at Michael, I suddenly felt the full flood of love. Of all the sights on this vast earth, this sight, the sight of his face across a table, was most beautiful to me. I felt the pull of the cosmic tides that had brought us together. I was beyond the draw of earth gravity. I was seeing us as two souls who had inhabited the vast blackness of space and made this rendezvous on earth. Yes, this was my heart's choice. Yes, this love that I was feeling was what made human birth worthwhile. I felt the frailness of this human life we had chosen together—so tenuous, so easily ended. As the baby's life was ebbing now, silently, in a deepening red pool of blood, so our lives could end at any time. And this made the love all the more precious.

We spoke of many things. As usual, we tried to assess our situation for the gains. This has always been Michael's way, and early in the pregnancy he had asked me to see what I was learning, so that if anything happened I would still have that. What I saw back then was that after the initial shock of losing my students passed, there had been a happy anticipation of being home once again and having time to be with him. "If this is how you feel," Michael had said, "perhaps you should take that time for us next year even if we don't have a baby." So that little piece of clarity was already in place. What else were we learning?

I was learning the frailty of human life and the power of love in the face of that frailty. But this was something to be lived, with no need for words.

Rather we discussed the lesson we were getting in timing. We had always been the kind of people to plan ahead. But slowly we were being weaned of that, trained to locate ourselves in the present. First there had been the expectation of a year teaching school. Then, when we learned that I was pregnant, we adjusted to the idea of my leaving school in February, just before the baby was due. Then, when the leak began, we realized I might have to leave in January. As time went on, it became Christmas we were holding out for, when the baby would first become viable even if born premature. And now we were hoping just to make it to Thanksgiving. But in view of the change in leaking just while we were here at the restaurant, even Thanksgiving was unlikely. As Michael observed, "We never know more than about the next four hours."

Michael confessed that he was relieved that the end seemed near. This was hard for him—hard to admit to himself and hard to say to me. But he had done more medical reading than I. He knew the relevant facts: If the baby were born soon, it would die. But if it were born later, it might suffer all sorts of damage, in body and mind, and he did not feel strong enough to welcome a child who was severely limited. Also, at the point where the baby became viable, all sorts of heroic medical measures would be pressed on me. Doctors would recommend massive amounts of steroids, and so on. We would be faced with hard decisions and, perhaps, a hard future.

I was surprised. I had not thought this far. I had read of damage from insufficient amniotic fluid and had sifted through the medical material for possible hints on how to prevent it. (There were none.) But I did not tolerate thoughts of abnormality, and I had not done reading on the problems of premature birth. I was simply working on the issues of strength and endurance. I was a donkey tied to the millstone.

Now I checked my feelings as we talked: No, all I could

find inside me was simple loyalty, that old allegiance I had been marveling at all week. I simply could not think ahead. I knew only that I could count on myself to maintain the life within me to the best of my ability. I felt a curious relaxation in my pelvic area when I thought about delivery. I knew that I would not push the baby out, that I would not contribute one jot to the early delivery of this baby. The soul who had chosen me was free to choose an early birth; I could not help that. But my will was unwavering: I would not willfully hasten that birth by the space of a single breath.

We talked also about life in general, and what was going to be "the next step" spiritually. I now realized that teaching school was not going to be my next step. I had taken the job to escape from the gnawing I had begun to suffer in my time alone at home. But the job had proved at least as distressing as the gnawing, though in a more creative way. I could now see that school teaching was off the track of my life's purpose, able at best to supply fuel but not direction. Having had the eight days at home, I realized I had been missing myself, losing something precious by my lack of time to meditate. If I were not going to raise a child next year, there must be something else. But what was it?

And through it all: the love. Time was going by, but not for me. I felt fulfilled. This *was* my life's purpose: to sit across from Michael and bathe in this love I felt. There was no reason that I could see ever to end it. What could I possibly move on to that would be more worthwhile? But Michael was practical, and he let me know that it was time for us to go.

This was a hard day for him, perhaps because he could not yet accept the relief he shared with me. For me it was wonderful. Everything connected with it acquired a glow. The restaurant is still special to me. And the blue shirt I wore that day I would choose again three days later, when I was feeling queer and uneasy, in great need of comfort—on the day that I gave birth.

I was back at school on Monday. I remember nothing of the day except for the constant leaking. After school I drove to the medical center for my appointment. I saw the same doctor who could not "prove" the rupture. And again, he could find nothing wrong. He said not to worry, the bleeding might be external and might just stop by itself. I did some food shopping, ran into a friend from the school of education and asked her if she knew any good replacement for me since

I would be leaving to have a baby. My words now seem strange to me. Was I hiding something from myself? Did I not know already that I would not be leaving school to raise a child?

As I drove home, I began to speak out loud to my "voice." Not that the voice was there; but my need was so great. "What would you have me do?" I pleaded. "Just tell me what to do, and you know I will do it." I knew the strength of my own will. I knew I could do whatever I was asked. But there was no response.

In my despair I addressed the soul of the baby. I felt old. I felt my forty-two years and my weariness. I thought of all the dedicated parents of handicapped children who did their utmost to compensate, and create for their children an atmosphere of love, hope, and empowerment. I did not feel up to the task. "Please," I said. "I welcome you, if you choose life, I support you in every way. But please, if you are to be born abnormal, reconsider. It seems such a hard life to me. I don't think we will be able to give you a good life. I'm sorry. But this seems to be beyond what we can do."

I was crying bitterly as I spoke. I never sensed a response. But somehow I felt listened to. And I felt relief. Later I wondered whether I had done what I thought I would never do: disinvite the baby. But no, it seemed to me that I had not so much disinvited it as simply acknowledged what is.

I went into the house while my family unpacked the groceries. I lay by the wood stove, tired. My parents telephoned to ask about Thanksgiving plans. Now that it was affecting our arrangements, I told them my news. And so they got to know that I was pregnant for the final days.

I was able to go to school on Tuesday. For twenty-four

hours I had been feeling pressure in the vaginal area which reminded me vaguely of the last stage of my earlier pregnancies. And now, on Tuesday, I felt intense weight and pressure low down, as if the baby's head were resting right there. I taught, ended the religion unit with a chart of those last dead facts, and went after school to the "maximum half hour" staff meeting which lasted an hour. I could feel the pregnancy withdrawing in a serious way. I wanted to leave the meeting, but what could I say? "Please, ladies and gentleman (the one male teacher), sitting here is not good for me. I can feel the life-force draining as you talk." For all I knew, I might last another month. There was simply no way to tell if this was really hurting the baby. And so I stayed, trying to enjoy the calmness of the atmosphere which Diane always created, even when the topics were pure paperwork and trivia.

I came home and lay down next to the wood stove, breathing heavily. It was strange. Rather than breathing, I was half panting. I got up long enough to eat a bit, then lay down next to the stove and continued panting for hours. At some point Michael's cousin Sandy, with whom he had not spoken for years, called to tell him she had just been accepted for in vitro fertilization and was flying to Virginia to begin the lab work. She was thirty-eight, desperate after ten years of trying to become pregnant, feeling that her life would not be complete without a baby.

I lay on the floor listening. It was another sour moment, another one of those impossible timings, but who could bear to count them any more? I remembered Genesis' words: "Smile. And know there are no accidents in the universe, and all is always perfectly timed." I could feel the forces of the universe rearranging themselves. I mentally addressed Sandy: "The life force is leaving me. Perhaps it will enter you. Who knows how these things work? If I could, I would send it over to you. And may you fare better."

I went to bed and lay there, breathing heavily still. I was having contractions, but not intense enough to keep me from sleep. In the middle of the night I woke in a total sweat, chilled. I changed nightgowns. Hours later I woke again, wet and chilled. There were more contractions, five minutes apart, but still not intense. I telephoned school to say that I would not be coming in to teach and then I called the doctor to make an appointment. Might I deliver this day? I felt strange and wanted every comfort possible. I went to the closet and instinctively my hand reached for the blue shirt I had worn at the restaurant with Michael—as if I could wrap myself in the warmth stored up there, as comfort against what was to come.

It was unfortunate timing. I had about ten appointments for parent conferences scheduled for the afternoon. I had not ruled out driving to school for them, and so I packed clothes for the conferences and drove myself to the doctor. Michael offered to drive me, but I knew I could do it. And besides, I wanted to keep my options open for parent appointments by taking my own car.

Just in case, Michael drove behind me most of the way, on his way to work. I was having contractions, but I took out my faithful tool, the mantra, and used that to get me through. Every once in a while I would have to slow the car down almost to a halt. "Remember this in the future," I told myself. "Don't be impatient when someone slows down." And I realized how this lesson applied to all of life. "Remember, don't be impatient with anyone. You never know what another person is going through." How could I forget that after today?

The doctor told me there was no dilation, but I did have a fever of one hundred and one degrees, a temperature which I had not reached in the last fifteen years. He said that if my fever rose, I should come back at once. He would then recommend that I go on to the hospital and be delivered.

Now I was faced with a decision. It was midmorning. I could wait a while and then drive to school for the conferences. I could go home and lie down in bed and forget everything. Or I could stay in town, in case, waiting to see if I would need to go back to the clinic.

I decided against driving to school and telephoned to say so. (Diane had wisely canceled my conferences already.) I was pulled towards home and the comfort of my own bed. But this would mean being alone until my son got home from school at three o'clock. And he would not be able to drive me if anything happened. I was no longer confident that I could drive myself.

I felt queer. That was the only way to say it. Ten years earlier my father-in-law died of ALS, a degenerative disease. He had never in his life complained about ailments or pain, and he did not with this disease either. But one day, getting into a taxi, he said, "I don't feel good"—and died minutes after. Like him, I had no words for what I was feeling. There was nothing to which I could compare it. If I were an animal I would have been moaning or pacing senselessly. I felt uneasy.

In the end it was mood, not mind, which made the decision—pure animal uneasiness. I went to my husband's office. I found a strip of rug and lay on the floor while he did his work and then went to meetings. I was alone most of the time, but at least I knew that people were nearby.

There were more contractions. They had been going on all morning and were gradually getting worse. I had promised myself that I would not contribute to an early delivery by pushing. I reviewed that promise and firmed my resolve.

At first it was easy. I could practically ignore the contractions just by saying mantra. But then the contractions got rougher. I learned that if I panted slightly I could stay relaxed through the contractions and dissipate their force. But after a while nothing worked: I could not relax through them no matter what I did. I was able to continue witnessing my pain, though, and that was a help. Noticing how unpleasant the contractions were, I wondered why: After all, I was not really *feeling* the pain so much as *watching* myself feel it; and watching anything should not be that bad.

All this took will, but it was subtle. I distracted myself by timing the contractions. And in between contractions I cast about mentally for new plans, knowing that I could not go on like this all day. But through it all, I was vigilant. If I could not relax any longer through my contractions, still I would not give in to them. I would not tell myself that the time for delivery was near. And I would not allow myself to want to push and get it over with. This was a measure of my loyalty, and it would long remain with me.

Months later, telling about the pregnancy and my commitment to the baby, I would still find tears filling my eyes when I got to the words, "And I never even pushed."

As the contractions got worse and worse, I realized I could not stay in Michael's office forever; a decision would have to be made. I did not want to go home, for that would have put me twenty minutes from the medical center and thirty-five from the hospital. I was dazed, and needed to be near help. I decided to go to the hospital and stay there until something was resolved. I telephoned the clinic and was told to stop there on my way to the hospital.

Meanwhile Michael was chairing a meeting. He has always had an uncanny sense of timing, and today was no exception. Following his intuition, he brought his meeting to an abrupt close and came back to his office, ready for us to go home. I told him that I had decided to go to the hospital, and said that I could drive myself. But this time he insisted on driving me.

Just as we approached the medical center, I had my first life-sized contraction. This one hurt. It was the real thing. It blocked out everything. For a moment I ceased to be. And when I came back to existence, I was in San Francisco in 1970 giving birth to my son. I was amazed. "So. All those memories are there, stored away, inaccessible until some twin awakens them." I could not move until this contraction was passed. Then, knowing my time was short between contractions, I raced into the building.

Usually I am absurdly timid when it comes to breaking rules. But now was no time for decorum. I rushed past the receptionist and called out to a nurse in the hall that I had to go to the bathroom. I walked into the nearest bathroom and sat down. The second real contraction was upon me. I intended to urinate, but it did not feel as if that were happening. I could swear that the baby's head—

Another time crunch! I was rocked by the impossibility. Thirty years ago, at age twelve, I was a junior counselor at a day camp. The counselors were quite a bit older than I, and I usually preferred to eat lunch with the children in my bunk. But one day I joined the counselors for lunch. They were talking about childbirth, and one of them, Wilma, was telling a story about her grandmother, who had always had her babies easily. The last baby, in fact, came out while she was going to the bathroom. "What did she do?" I asked. Wilma's answer: "She just pulled up her underpants to catch the baby's head."

I had never believed that story. I thought either Wilma or her grandmother had made it up. But there it was, filed in the "impossible stories" file and retrieved now, when it was happening in my own life.

I poked my head out the bathroom door and called to the nurse, "I could swear the baby's head is coming out." Perhaps she was used to these things. "Hurry!" she said. "Just pull up your pants and come to the examination room." I did just that.

I was on the table and the urge to push was there. I must do it. The head was already partially out. At last. I let myself push. And now the head was out. The relief was so intense that for a moment I *was* pure relief, had no other identity. And for the next twenty-four hours, just by moving my attention to that area, I could feel a flood of relief, any time. "Is the baby out?" I asked. "Yes, the head is out. Now push the rest." I pushed, and it was over.

And now for the "holy of holies." The darshan. The epiphany. I can remember from my early teens reading a book review in an underground newspaper that contained the word "epiphany" and its definition. "Epiphany: the sudden revelation and appearance of a divine being; a spiritual event in which the essence of something appears, as in a sudden flash of recognition." The word took my fancy, and I recorded it in a special notebook. I did not dream that I would one day be participating in an epiphany all my own. Or did

I? Is there not an inner knowing that knows the future all unknown?

Now I have come to the moments of epiphany. Afterrwards, for days, when asked about the birth, I could only close my eyes and repeat the words, "So beautiful. It was so beautiful." I wrote notes to the few friends who might understand, saying, "I would not have chosen to miss this. It was so beautiful." How could I explain?

And yet I must explain this beauty. You, whom I call the Golden Lady, this beauty was you. Approaching you, I am in a state of joy and fear. Finally I have reached the moments of your visit; now I am where I always longed to be. And yet I feel a despair. So swiftly your visit will be told. It will seem to have come and gone, dwarfed by the pages of background and aftermath. But it is this, your visit, your incredible darshan, that lasted less than a day, that gives life and meaning to the rest.

The telling will be too swift. I fear I will not be able to convey what you have offered me. How can I prolong the telling? How can I show the full freight of the love you brought with you?

I feel my words must sound a fanfare, as when the queen approaches. But your presence was silence, and my words are noisy. And so how can I use words to announce you?

I feel my words must be a ring to hold your diamond presence in a setting so that all may see. But Lady, you do not need my words. Your silence and your radiance are sufficient unto you.

Ah, it is we humans who need the ring. We are so accustomed to dismissing what lies in the dust of ordinary experience. If the diamond is not set in a ring, we may pass it by as glass, not recognizing it at all. It is we who need the words.

Weeks before, trying to repair my damaged tissues, I constructed an oriole nest for a baby. So now, painfully, toilfully, I attempt to weave a nest for you. I weave a nest to catch your presence. I weave a ring to show your light.

I know, Lady, that I can do neither. And yet I must try. What else are we humans born for?

Your diamond presence, did I say? No, Lady. Diamond is right only because it is so precious. But diamond is too cold. You were not white and brilliant like a diamond. You were soft and golden. You warmed like the sun, but you were not the sun. You were the source. If the sun is warm, it draws its warmth from you.

I did not see your light but felt it. Every cell of my body knows that your light was golden. There was a vibrance in the room, the steady hum of love, so that every part of me felt bathed. I know that bath and I know that light: it was golden.

Lady, Lady, lend me some of your light now, so my words may tell of you.

*T*he baby is out. It is over!

(But, ah, it has just begun.)

I am stunned. It has come to this. The delight, the weeks of suffering, the endurance: it has come to this. The baby is out. And we all know this early birth means death.

I see the doctor and two nurses standing over me. I lift my head to look at the baby, who is lying on my belly. She is so beautiful: dark-haired, with eyes still fused shut, fingers and toes perfect. She shows no damage from any loss of fluid. She is delicate, but she is perfect and complete.

She gives a faint cry. This beautiful, pink, and perfect person, who never shows any real distress, never complains or cries out for help: she gives a faint cry. She is at peace, and her cry puts me at peace, too.

This is no lusty cry of opening to life. This is no petulant cry of pain or need, no asking to be held or fed. This is just the weakest and gentlest of hellos. A being has just wafted down to earth, a being fragile and light as a dandelion puff. She lands with no pain and gives a mild cry of surprise and delight. "Ah, planet Earth." She has reached her destination and is ready.

The room has already become hushed as any cathedral. And her cry does not disrupt the silence. Nor does the medical drama, which unfolds in its quiet way, a leitmotif against the silence.

It has not occurred to me that I can hold her. I am passive, waiting for "them" to take her away. But it is our fortune that I never reached the hospital. For in this clinic there are no heroic measures available, no special medical units to which she can be rushed off.

At some point one of the nurses wraps her in a blanket. As if she were a normal baby.

Her heartbeat is slow, they say. Well, how could it be otherwise?

Her lungs are not fully formed, they say. She cannot breathe well enough.

The doctor has called the hospital to send an ambulance. As if anything can be done to save this life. It is a gentle fiction that we all are keeping up. But we all know she will die. The air is filled with the hum of her presence, and that hum spells love and death at once.

A nurse has lifted her and set her on my breast. She gives a few more delicate cries, each one weaker than the last. Her cries are beautiful. There is no lovelier sound I shall ever hear.

The room is our cathedral and her cries blend with the silence. The room is vibrating with love and her sound melts into the love.

There is no desire in that sound, no reproach. She does not want milk or holding or comfort. Those cries are her briefest salutation to us, and to the planet Earth.

It is not just that her lungs are too weak for more. She is utterly at peace, and those cries announce her peace to us, impart her peace to us.

So beautiful. So utterly at peace.

Time has stopped, and I can hear the mantra going on within me. I am at peace. The world is at peace. There is total stillness in the room. And you are beautiful.

Lady, it is you. If you are the baby on my breast, you are also the silence in the room, the love filling the room, the light, the golden melting warmth that can be felt more than seen.

Om namah shivaya. Om namah shivaya. The mantra speaks itself inside me. The room seems to be made of mantra, the walls of vibration only. It is not for any purpose, not to comfort or to succor the baby on my breast, not to calm myself or be still. The mantra is just commentary: and you are the text.

So beautiful. So unutterably beautiful.

And what to say in the face of such beauty? Om namah shivaya. What else is there to say?

I bow to the beauty of this universe.

I bow to the beauty of this universe, to all the beauty that is in potential and will never come to fruit or flower.

I bow to the beauty of this universe, to all the beauty that is in potential and that will never come to fruit or flower, and to this infant, to this beauty and this life leaving, this thing that was never meant to be.

I bow to the cruel and beautiful law that says it must be so. We humans have such hunger for it: for the beautiful, for the sacred, for love. What is this, this mysterious law, this beautiful law, that witholds, that withdraws, that makes the visit just long enough for us to sense the possible, then mercilessly cuts it off?

Om namah shivaya. Om namah shivaya. I am not saying mantra to save my soul or buy my freedom. I am not saying mantra to protect this baby. Whoever this mysterious visitor is, I know she has no need of protection. She is at one with what is happening, totally at peace with herself and the grand design into which this all fits.

No, I am not saying mantra at all. The mantra is saying itself. The universe is commenting on its own perfection.

The cries are stilled, for the baby cannot take in enough air to sustain them. A tiny oxygen mask is given her. And a nurse notices that she must be cold and, almost as an afterthought, puts a tiny hat upon her head. As if she were a normal newborn child, with a life ahead of her. They are treating her with full respect.

The medical leitmotif continues, never intrusive. Against the beauty and the silence, the medical people have been making their moves. Doctors have been paged from elsewhere in the clinic. By now there are about nine medical people in the room.

But the stillness is never broken. All of the people here are hushed and reverent, as if at the birth of a savior.

I remember a sermon about the birth of Jesus: the heavens were rent and angels were heard singing glory to God. It was not that the angels were singing glory because Jesus was born, the minister was careful to explain: angels are always singing glory to God. It was just that on this one occasion the heavens were opened, so their song could be heard.

So now, for these precious moments, the heavens are rent. Your song can be heard, Lady. And your song is love, light, and stillness. If medical minds are thinking about oxygen and ambulances, hearts are not. The hearts can hear your song.

All the medical people are reverent, in awe. It can be known from the angle of the bodies, the sorrow in the voices, the peace in the eyes. They, too, recognize the holy when it is here.

It only seems they came to help at your birth. But I know, Lady: they have come to see you, to feel your love.

No one is ever intrusive or brusque. Just incredible peace, beauty, sorrow.

So beautiful. So unutterably beautiful.

Michael has been sitting in a chair nearby. Now the blond nurse—one I have never seen before, who seems to have appeared just for this birth—lifts the baby and gives her to Michael to hold, saying, "She's your little girl."

These words wrench us, but they enrich us, too. We are grateful for the experience they allow.

Michael holds the baby. His tears are heavy. But there is silence everywhere. Not the silence of no sound; the full, rich silence of love vibrating all around.

❧

An ambulance has been called, but the pediatrician says it is hopeless. There is just the waiting. And all the while, the song, the hum of love.

Her death is as delicate as her birth. There is no protest or good-bye.
    She dies—if that is the word; it seems she never chose to live—in Michael's arms. No one knows when. First it had been hard to find a heartbeat. And now it is impossible.
    That is all.

The request for an ambulance is cancelled. And then, as softly as they had been present, the medical people disappear.

And then we are alone in the room.
The two of us.
And you.

We are alone in the stillness.

Michael and I cry. It is all so beautiful. It has all been so beautiful. What are we crying for? Is it for the loss of a life? Or is our crying simply the soul's way of greeting your beauty, of saying hello and good bye at once?

The everyday world somehow manages to reassert itself, but quietly, gently, without ever disturbing us from our beautiful dream. Somehow, with words that are soft and *slow, with words that can reach out across galaxies to unite us in this bond of everyday reality, we manage to decide to order a pizza for dinner. It is not that we are hungry. We could not be; we have not quite returned to our bodies yet. But we know the children will want dinner. And so, from that very room, we telephone the pizza parlor to make our order, our home to tell Joshua what has happened, and the ballet school to leave word for Elena that we will be late.*

These tasks are accomplished by Michael. I am still lying on the examining table, which has so recently become the delivery table.

We are still caught in a zone of no-time, and yet, there is time. Every moment is eternally long, but there are moments, and we know that they are bringing us to the point when we will drive to pick up pizza and then drive to the ballet school to take Elena home.

Home. That place has always been so comforting. But now it pales beside the home that we are in. Here, where we are, where you are still pouring out your golden light, we are home. We are home as we can never be elsewhere. This stillness, this love, this timelessness is our home. There is no place that would draw us from here.

The doctor returns. There are arrangements to be made. We have assumed that this infant is ours, this tiny being who weighs no more than a pound. But no, she falls under the aegis of the law. We must now dispose of her body in a legal manner. My husband questions the doctor. "You mean we cannot take her home and bury her?" The doctor makes a telephone call to the coroner and says no.

For a moment there is a quiet confrontation, with challenge on one side and sympathy on the other. Michael looks the doctor fully in the eye and slowly asks, "And what if we do take her home?"

There is silence. Then the doctor answers, just as slowly, "I would not stop you." And after a moment he adds, "But make sure you bring her to the funeral home tomorrow morning."

Is this his consolation to us? Or is it a relief to have this body removed from the clinic, a place where, after all, a dead body is an embarrassment, a proof of failure, a defeat of medical hopes?

Michael and I are pleased. Our treasure remains with us. This small and beautiful body seems somehow to have been the source that broadcast the love and silence that envelop us. To us this body is still alive with that vibration.

It is all so beautiful. Still so beautiful.

The nurse returns and helps me get ready to go. In the confusion of the birth, my underpants have been thrown out. She gives me a large diaper to wear. Even in my sorrow I smile at the irony: I have come in to have a baby, and now I walk out like an overgrown baby myself.

Two hours have gone by. Two hours. I cannot take it in. We would never have known. Time had no meaning. There was never any sense of passage of time, just a few vividly remembered "nows" and the fullness of the darshan.

We walk out through the waiting room. I am carrying the baby in my arms, as if she were alive. None of the mothers-to-be in the waiting room will ever know, will ever be upset *by the sight of their worst fears come true. It is not that I am fooling them. I, too, am held in this gentle fiction. There is life, warmth, and comfort in my arms.*

I look at the mothers, some of them with children. I expect to feel some envy or some bitterness. Instead, to my surprise, I feel a welling up of benevolence, a curious sense of release. I recognize this sort of release. I first experienced it years ago, on the day when I stopped clinging to my youth. I remember it all perfectly.

I was in my early thirties; I stopped at a stop sign, when a radiant young woman crossed in front of my car. I steeled myself for the usual distressing self-comparison and found instead, to my delight, a release and a rising of goodwill. It was as if I were God dispensing roles, well pleased with my ever-shifting choices: "Yes, I need some young, some middle, and some old. You are taking one of the young parts for me. Paula is no longer able to; she is doing middle now." When I returned to myself, I was still feeling the goodwill, and I sent the young woman some silent appreciation: "Ah, I'm glad you're so attractive. I like to see you people parading around with your rather raw but dazzling energy. I cannot do that any longer. Thank you for doing it for me."

So now, walking through the waiting room, carrying in my arms this baby who will never be a child, I mentally address the women there: "I am so glad that there are still some of you around who can perpetuate this human race. It seems that I no longer can." Once more the gates of kinship are being thrown open: another marvel in the series of marvels that have been this pregnancy. And in a flash I understand the reason for the Greek tradition mentioned by Socrates, that midwives must be themselves past the age of bearing: so that there could be this quality of unrestrained goodwill.

We walk to the car. There is such warmth in carrying this baby with us. It does not feel like a dead thing at all. There is simply intense darshan.

In the car we escort our precious cargo, first to the pizza parlor and then to the ballet school. We talk, but still softly, gently, as if we do not want to rouse our sleeping baby, but really because we do not want to rouse ourselves from the enchantment.

We discuss whether to unwrap our precious bundle to show the baby to Elena. After all, it is by ordinary standards a dead body, to which the conditioned response would be fear or disgust. And also, it might scare Elena, make her fearful for her own future pregnancies. But on the other hand, this is something exquisite, something holy, something utterly real and beyond time. And we have always shared our spiritual treasures with our daughter; it is hard to stop that now.

In the end, we cannot fight the urge to share, to be generous with the holy. When Elena gets into the car, we ask her whether she would like to see the baby, and she answers yes.

When we get home, we ask Joshua, and he, too, wants to see the baby. We warm the pizza in the oven, and I go upstairs to the attic to look for a container for the baby.

Our attic is large and full of odds and ends. I have a feeling there must be something there. Softly I pad around the attic, my hand reaching tentatively to piles, like a dowsing rod. And in the end, I find what we need. For the opening of the Dome of Peace a Buddhist monk had given Elena a *beautiful twelve-inch statue of the Buddha. We set the statue on a table in our hallway. And the box had been so cunningly made, so lovingly made, that we could not bring ourselves to throw it out. We put it in the attic.*

Here it is: wooden and delicate, with a sliding panel to seal it and with beautiful Japanese calligraphy along one side, characters that must be naming the Buddha. The size fits exactly. But more than that, the whole mood of the box fits exactly: it was made to house the holy.

I bring the box down. Michael was planning to make a crude pine box himself, not wanting to place the baby in an anonymous box made by a stranger. When he sees what I am carrying, he feels a shock of recognition: this is our box.

We lay the baby gently in her container, taking our last looks. Michael asks, "Would it be all right if we laid the baby on the puja table?" This is the small table before which we sit to meditate, used to hold objects which call forth our reverence and bring us to a deeper meditation.

We look at each other. We each know what the question means and what the answer is: Yes, this box, with its contents, belongs on that table. It is as sacred to us as anything has ever been.

We lay the box on the table and light candles on either side of it. And for a while we sit with you, staring into the dark, feeling some of your stillness.

We come downstairs for dinner and reestablish contact with our children. And after a while we bring the box out to the car, so that its contents will stay cool overnight. We yield this much: that the body is subject to the laws of decay. We know that we have been in the presence of the eternal. But we know also that the eternal has borrowed a phys-

ical form for the occasion. And we choose to slow the process of decay.

As I lie in bed that night, there is a real holding to Michael. If losing the baby was enormous, how much more so, how unthinkable, would it be to lose him?

"So beautiful. So unutterably beautiful." I hear these words in my mind whenever I think about the baby. And they hold true for Michael, too. And for this love I feel between us.

I woke up the next morning with a singular thought: "I am not pregnant." How remarkable. And yet, does not the whole world operate by this principle? One moment one is hungry, the next not. One moment one is sleeping, the next not. One moment one is happy, married, has found the path; the next not. Some changes in my life I had fought, others embraced. Would I embrace this one?

I asked to make breakfast for the children. It had been so

long since I could do things. The sense of physical relief was still with me from the delivery. And also the sense of joy at being able to move around freely again. I had never let myself see how hard it was. But now, now that I could stand and walk at will, I realized what I had suffered. It had been so long since I could wash dishes or make a meal. These were luxuries to me now.

The children left for school. I called my school to say what had happened and surprised myself by crying. We called the funeral home. If we could not bury the baby on our own land, then we would have the body cremated. This way we could at least scatter her ashes here. We made an arrangement to come in later in the morning.

I washed my hair and did the laundry, to set a symbolic boundary, to wall off the birth and death. As I went about my tasks, an ancient Greek maxim kept arising in my mind: *Nekues koprion ekbletoteroi*—"Corpses are more to be thrown out than dung." Being unsentimental, I had always accepted this view, and had admired the Greek language, able to express it in a mere three words. But now I mused on its meaning. This body that was temporarily in my care was not garbage. It was to be thrown into the earth as ashes, yes, but for enrichment. By an odd twist, I saw the literal truth of the Greek maxim, appropriate for our compost-conscious age: Bodies are more to be thrown out than dung, not because they are worthless but because they are worth *more*, giving more enrichment to the earth.

Meanwhile Michael was outside chopping wood—or so it seemed. His real purpose was something other. The wood-pile was near the car, in which the baby was residing. Later he told me that all the while he chopped wood, he was leaning inwardly toward the car, intensely aware of the power source inside it, of the presence emanating from it. This was his way of staying with the darshan.

I was unaccountably slowed down as I washed my hair and hung the laundry. I did not want to arrive late at the funeral home, but I felt unable to rush. It would be improper to hurry—as if I were transacting business and not performing sacred acts. It would be dishonoring that beautiful being. Finally I was ready.

I had been pleased at how well taken care of the baby was: wrapped in her blanket and housed in her perfect box. The blanket had been new, given to her with love and care, her only earthly gift. But this morning I remembered that there was a little stain on the blanket, perhaps a spot of her excrement. I did not want to let her go up in smoke with that stain, and meant to stop at a fabric store near the funeral home and buy some new clean cloth.

As we drove in I told Michael that I wanted to stop to buy some cloth. I planned to buy you silk, a beautiful shroud of white silk, knowing no gift would be too precious for you. This silk would match your purity and make my final statement: "You, who were with us yesterday, whoever you are, you were so pure, your presence so perfect. Only a spotless garment can suit your spotless being." To me it seemed reasonable, admirable even, to use money in order to speak truth. But the language of symbolism did not come easily to Michael, and I thought he might protest, finding it an absurd waste to buy something that would soon go up in smoke.

He agreed to stop, and we went to a natural fabric store, where I surveyed all the silk. None matched my expectation for luster. Finally I settled on some pure white linen for the shroud. I bought almost a yard, which turned out to be an enormous amount. I had not remembered how small the baby was.

I thought we would wrap the baby ourselves, but Michael did not want to. He was sure of his feelings, and he explained them to me: He had a perfect image of the baby, warm and lovely as it was born, and he did not want to see what time and decay had done.

"Is" arose in my mind, that simple word, as it often does when I find myself avoiding the truth. I have learned to be an explorer of "is." If time and decay had spoiled that lovely form, then I might as well find out. And I wanted to be with you one last time. Whatever had happened, you would always be beautiful for me. And this was part of it all.

But I yielded to Michael's feelings. I wanted to stay in unison with him on everything concerning the baby. I was pleased that he had gone along with my wish to buy the cloth. And now I agreed to forego this final darshan. We would ask the funeral director to wrap her in the linen.

We went into the funeral home. Tears streamed from my eyes as we discussed the details. When it was time to mention the new shroud, Michael asked me, "Do you want to wrap the baby?" I was surprised, having resigned myself to our decision. But he asked again, "Do you want to wrap the baby?" I knew this meant he wanted to.

And so we did.

We went to the room where the bodies are prepared.

We are in the preparation room. A cold room, empty except for a long gray marble slab with a little well at one end, to catch fluids. There is a pair of surgical steel scissors lying on the slab. Nothing in this room speaks of life.

~

We open the box, sliding out the wooden panel, and hold the baby one more time. Cautiously we unwrap the blanket.

She is still lovely. Time and decay have done nothing to her. She is a little redder, that is all.

And cold. So cold. How can a human be so cold? The box feels warm, but her body is as chilling as the marble.

We throw away the soiled blanket. We notice that the plastic clamp is still around her umbilical cord. She won't need that. We cut off the extra cord and throw away the plastic clamp.

We wrap her in her white shroud.

She is so lovely. Still so beautiful. So unutterably beautiful.

She sheds her silvery silence around us. Not so golden this time. Not vibrant love, but stillness as in death. A total purity. And this is the moonlight of love. We cannot bear to leave this love.

We are both crying. For me she sums up all the lost potential of the world, all the beauty that might have been but was never meant to be, all the beauty that the world is crying out for. We cannot bear to leave her.

I feel the marble coolness of her cheek. Ah, so cold. That coldness draws a blade of pain across my heart. It sets the final seal, lets me know that for all our human hopes and feelings, the law remains immutable. The beauty of this world is limited: so much and no more.

I stroke her head several times so that my fingers may memorize her curve. We take our last looks.

This figure draped in white impresses itself upon me. It enters deep. Its full meaning is not known. But there is stillness here, and purity. There is love and (ah, so cold) finality. For me this will be the strongest darshan of all.

Michael will always remember the warm and lovely being whom he held on his lap as she took her faint last breaths. But for me it will be this cold, white-shrouded loveliness. I ask myself why. Is Michael drawn more to life, and I to death? I do not know. I know only that this figure draped in white seems to give me the final message, carries the fullest weight of meaning and of love.

We shut the box.

When we emerged, the funeral director asked me to fill out some forms. We had no name for the baby. But when I came to the space for the baby's name, I was overwhelmed by a sense of loss, by my longing for all the beauty that you represented, all the beauty that could never be. I could not accept the finality after all. I could not accept this death sentence on the world. And so I wrote "Not Yet" for the name. This was too unconventional for the director, I suppose. For when the ashes were returned to us days later, the name remained a blank.

We left the funeral home and did errands together. We returned the books on pregnancy to the library. We bought a new toaster at the local shopping mall. I could feel the mall dulling me. I fought the dulling; I did not want to lose the special feeling of your darshan. But I knew that there was mercy in the dulling, too. It would have to come.

We went to a restaurant to eat. How many landmarks in our life these restaurant talks have been. We talked about the pregnancy, trying to take in the whole of it. And I heard Michael's words as a soothing myth—a myth which, if I did not know you, did not know that you are not a limited human soul—I would still hold as mine today.

"Imagine a very advanced soul," Michael said, "who wants to try an experiment, to test itself in a very advanced way. It wants to see whether it can stay conscious, hold on to its intention to remain discarnate, through a birth and death. After all, what are the seventy years in between? To an advanced soul, they may be as dust. Maybe it's the birth and death that are most potent. And the soul wants to experience only these."

Yes, I am listening. Go on, Michael. Your words comfort me. Your very pace and stillness comfort me. Go on with your story.

"So the soul goes searching for some recipients. 'Let's see,' it says. 'I could choose some people who really want a baby and who have some bad karma coming to them. Then I will wipe them out with sorrow at my leaving, and they will be scarred for life.'

"'But no,' it says. 'I want to do the experiment, but I don't want to leave two scarred human beings. What can I do? Hmmm, I see the perfect couple . . .'

"And so the soul chose us."

What a soothing story. What a comforting myth—so comforting that I would tell it as a bedtime story to my daughter.

And yes, it made sense. We *would* be the logical choice: We would not hold the soul here, would not lure it by incredible desire, nor bind it by resistance to its death. We had cooperated in every way, offering ourselves as the theater of action. And we were grateful for the gift. Not only for the darshan, but for the other gifts as well: the chance to grow closer, test ourselves, appreciate each other the more; and the chance to learn.

And all those signatures, Michael went on, all those impossibilities: Did they not confirm the myth? One would be enough, two if we were slow. But all of these? The impossible conception, the timing of the rupture, the Bushman story of the amniotic fluid, even that call from cousin Sandy? Yes, you left us clues enough for consolation, it was true. It always *did* seem to be your decision, not ours, both to be conceived and then to disincarnate. And we were not scarred or wasted by that decision, just moved by the purity, the beauty, the darshan, and the sorrow.

I had always found it silly when people resisted the word "die," using euphemisms like "passed away." But with you, Lady, I could understand it. It is not just that your eternal presence was beyond time, could not have a beginning or an end. It is also that *as* the baby, you simply did not die. You left the body too lightly for us to use that word. You shed that delicate body as lightly as any of us has ever shed a sweater in the summer. There was no rip in the fabric of existence. You died as gently as you were born.

I remembered now saying to Genesis that love was what would make it worth incarnating. He had voiced agreement. "Yes, it is," he said. But he had added these strange words: "It is also true that that is why you disincarnate."

Ah, so he knew. Of course. You proved him right. You brought us as much love in your leaving as in your coming. You were made of love. If you chose to disincarnate, it could only have been for the sake of going toward a greater love.

We finished lunch and went back for dessert to the restaurant where I had worn the blue shirt. We talked more there. I was feeling so much love for Michael, as on that other day. I felt how much more important to me he was than all else, even than the baby. To be with him in this lifetime: how enormous.

The image of the white-shrouded figure kept coming back to me, and with it the word "karmaless." The law of karma: the force that draws a soul back again and again for birth, so that it may experience the consequences of its acts. This baby had no karma. She may have taken birth as an experiment, or else as a gift of grace to us. But she had not been called to earth by any need to reap the rewards or punishment for previous acts.

This could be felt from the very moment of her birth. She expressed no desire when she landed lightly on the earth, just the mildest surprise. And she involved herself in no network of desires during her brief stay. She asked for nothing and she complained of nothing. She was without karma the duration of her earthly existence. She was pure.

Sometimes a new parameter enters my mind, and without trying I find myself using it to scan people. First it was consciousness. I would look into the eyes I met and ask inwardly, "Have you been blazed in the fire of truth? Do you know how small our everyday selves are in comparison to our true expanse?" Then I began to look for the quality of inner peace, or stillness. After that it was life-force. And now, suddenly, there is a new one: "Are you karmaless? Or are you heading that way?"

I scanned everyone coming into the restaurant. There were some individuals who seemed lighter than others, who seemed to be carrying less baggage of karma with them and creating less as they went along. Right here at lunch, some people sitting at the tables were getting deeper and deeper enmeshed in their network of desires and aversions, while others were staying clear.

I scrutinized Michael. His face was still, his eyes at peace. His stillness gave him an element of that quality of being karmaless. I scanned my memory: Who else? Ah, the Buddhists at the Dome of Peace. Were they not living with reduced karma? And was this not part of their "largeness"? I pictured Clara, the Buddhist nun, with her clean-shaven head and innocent smile. She even *looked* like a newborn babe! How had I never noticed?

And through it all the image—of a tiny figure, shrouded in white.

Michael reminded me that it was time for us to leave. He needed to be dropped off at his office for some work. And I needed to drive home now if I was going to be there for my children when they got off the school bus—a rare event this year.

For me, I would never have left. I was still in perfect communion with Michael. And somehow this lunch, of all the many, had not reached consummation. Michael agreed, remarking that this seemed to be a pattern with aging: less consummation, even in simple things like eating and sleep. But time was going by, and it was time for us to leave.

On my way home I must have entered the baby's space of not quite incarnating—or at least of not incarnating willingly. For as I drove home, I found myself rebelling: "No, I refuse. I do not want to, I do not consent to live in this world of clocks and schedules, of school buses and dinner times."

But a voice, gently chiding, spoke to me: "Rules of the game, rules of the game."

I knew what the voice was telling me. If that seed of communication were expanded, this is what the voice would say: "If you want this love, if you want to be in communion with your husband, to share this life with your children, to teach your students, then you have to accept time. It is the condition of the world you have chosen to inhabit. In *this* world, if you do not get home on time, you will not be there when the school bus comes. It is that simple."

As for the other choice, ah! I knew that one: to leave this world, to disincarnate, as the baby did.

And once again, I am seeing the image—that lovely figure, shrouded in white.

We woke early the next morning, at 4:30. We lay together, taking comfort from each other. Holding Michael, I
found myself seeing the image of the baby, that lovely figure
in white. And for a moment I was not sure which one I was
holding. And then a voice said to me, "Your husband is as
beautiful as this baby. So just hold to him."

After a while I got up to meditate.

I am in the blue church once again. There are niches in the walls, with images set in them, flickering with the light of oil lamps. My corridor is off to the left.

I walk down.

Slowly I breathe, slowly I count from one to ten. On the tenth inbreath I panic. I have been feeling cramps from the birth, and it seems to me I cannot leave my body behind if I am feeling cramps.

"You will be through," I assure myself. "The cramps don't prove anything. You can go from the physical feeling of cramps to the thought in the mind of cramps."

The outbreath comes, and ah! Now all is thought.

It is strange. No matter how lost or immersed I seem to be in my physical existence, there is always some perceptible "lightening" at this first door.

I quickly count another ten.

I am there already. This door does not take a shove or even a thought—just a whirling of the head, or one round nod, and I am through. No sense of passage even.

But now: the baby!

I am carrying the baby. I have the sense of strong arms, clothed in white, carrying the baby. My arms. I sense only shoulders and arms, nothing else. And cradled in those anonymous arms, the baby, shrouded in white.

Wait! I am the baby now, being held securely in those arms. And I, the baby, am holding fast. Holding fast to my decision not to live? To remain in the realms where I have always been?

I hold fast. I am just a point. I have no body. No mind. I have no mind. But I have intent. Without body, without mind, I still have my intent.

I hold fast. I hold fast to my intent. I am intent only. I go to ten. And then—so easy . . .

Like being born.

Two pushes (two breaths?) and I am out: into the light, into the peace of dying and death.

So: this was the baby's death? A birth into—this! A being born to greater light.

I have done it. I am in a new realm, a realm of light. This is where my teacher is supposed to be. "Well," I say, "I can't hear you."

I stop to listen.

"You are here by the use of mere intention. Just as with the baby."

I know this voice. It is the one I call the Explainer. The voice continues: "In fact, your way of carrying the baby was an exercise. You carried it with mere intention. Never did you allow yourself to will with the strength of desire. You kept thoughts of delivery from yourself at all times and never intended to deliver until delivery was in process. Your intent was pure and unwavering. So it must be—and merest intent only—to get through that door."

Thoughts recur. Shall I fight them? But have I not been thinking all along? And had I not been thinking, would I know what the voice said?

I sit reviewing, trying to remember all that has happened. The voice continues: "You are deciding whether or not to take the path of remembrance. That is your choice to make. There is some cost to remembering. But the decision is a generous one. For remembrance is the path of love.

"I cannot ever advise against what is generous and loving. But you may also wish, at some other time, to take the path of forgetting, and simply stay here in these realms."

I am torn. Thinking is happening, but I am fighting it. I try to go back to the blue church and start again, but I cannot.

I did choose the path of remembering: Why not write what I have heard?

I went back to bed. Using a flashlight under the covers, so the light would not disturb Michael, I wrote down what I remembered.

Michael and I went downstairs to begin our morning routine. The children came down for breakfast, then left for the school bus. When we were alone again, I told Michael about my morning meditation.

Michael had put up a pot of beans on the stove. He was going upstairs to shower when the beans boiled over. "Oh darn!" he called out, with some heat. "I considered telling you to turn them down, but I thought it could wait." Michael is a person who turns most of life's tasks into challenges. Whether pulling up at a traffic light or shoveling snow or talking with a stranger, he is usually aware that there is a choice to make, a chance to practice discipline toward perfection. I usually admire the positive aspects of his attitude. But this moment I heard only the element of self-blame.

And suddenly I am seeing the image—of the baby, clad in white.

"Forgive yourself," I said to Michael. I was trying to say what I was seeing, trying to *say* the baby.

What my words meant was: "Life is precious. We are all precious. And we are here so short a time. Take care of what you have, including yourself. There is no place for anger here, no matter how slight. Let it all be."

Michael went to shower. I scarcely knew what to do with myself. I was still in an exalted state from your visit, which had lasted so long. I wanted to stay in that state and yet take the path of remembering.

My familiar roles had all dissolved and had not yet crystallized again. I did not want to assume any of them. If I cleaned house, I might become a housewife again. If I prepared schoolwork, I might become a teacher again. I wanted to stay with you. I was like those pious Jews who love Queen Sabbath and try to keep her with them until long after sundown, finally admitting defeat with the sweet-smelling ceremony of *havdalah*, the swinging of spice and silver.

I longed to keep you with me, to make your visit last forever. But it came time to admit that your visit was over and secular life was beginning again. And I would use words to make my ceremony of separation: I began to type some notes about the birth.

⌁

My hands were limp, almost unable to press the keys. There was a state of relaxation, complete peace, as after any event of grace. And yet the seeds of sorrow were there, too. I typed:

"So. How little my hands want to move to this. Or is it just the lingering numbness from this morning's meditation?

"The baby. That holy-of-holies, not to be touched by this writing. The images: of the baby warm, pink, totally at peace, lying on my belly, taking her weak breaths. So beautiful.

"And in Michael's arms, where she must have taken her last breath. So beautiful.

"And then in the funeral home. Expecting worse, but the beauty unchanged. Still so beautiful. But this time so cold, so final."

As I typed, I remembered what the naturalist from Costa Rica wrote: The experiences now most alive for him are the ones he did not try to preserve in words or photographs. Is this a warning to me? Is something tarnished, lost, in the attempt at preservation?

I must not spoil anything. I must remember: Words surround only, do not penetrate or define. They are the fence around the fence.

"The baby. The wall of speculations. The wall of history. The attempts to learn. All nothing. The image: that is what is with me."

The image. Never to be forgotten.
And the words to seal it off, the only words which I would

use in comment for the longest time: "So beautiful. So beautiful."

I spent the day journaling. I suppose it was my way of mourning: trying to remember, trying to understand. I looked up events on the calendar, found old hastily written notes. And by the end of the day I had typed about twenty pages, not knowing they would someday be the kernel of a book.

When I was finished I felt ready to return to my job, ready to resume my roles and join with others in this common enterprise called life.

That night, putting Elena to sleep, I remembered the comforting myth that Michael had told me in the restaurant, about the soul's choosing us for its venture into life and a quick death. This tale became a bedtime story now.

I thought that the pregnancy had run its course, that the event was complete, rounded off, and that there would be no more suprises. But I was wrong. There was one last twist, a twist so odd and unexpected, so impossible, uncomfortable, and plain embarrassing, that I hardly know how to tell it. Just remembering it makes me squirm; I feel as if a paradox were lodged in my throat. And indeed, it *is* a paradox. For I know it to be true and false at once. It is true because the facts confirm it. But it is false because if it were true, it would make a mockery of all that came before, would turn all our human suffering into sham.

It was 2:30 the next morning, and I woke up needing to use the bathroom. I left our room quietly so as not to wake Michael. What a relief not to be worrying about leaking! This was only my third morning, and I was still not used to the relaxation of it all.

As I walked into the bathroom, I had a shocking thought: If the baby had been born normal, with a full childhood ahead, that worrying would still be with me. Oh, not leaking exactly. But yes, leaking. I would have been leaking for years with the unnamed anxieties of motherhood. "Is the baby all right? Does the baby need milk?" And then, "Will the world last? Will the baby have a good future? Be a good person?" And so on—forever it seemed. Suddenly I saw what it was to have a child: to submit to this constant leaking, to agree to feed this subterranean stream of worry, which drained one's energy without one's even knowing it. Did it ever end? My own children were still too young for me to find out.

Michael had teased me for being such a "volunteer." Soon after the leak began I had told him that I could manage if he went away for a week-long workshop. I had considered coming in to school for parent appointments on the day of the birth. And I had even volunteered to drive myself minutes before the birth. But yes, I was the ultimate volunteer. Without realizing it, I had just volunteered for at least another twenty years of worry, of preoccupation for the future of another.

For the first moment since the pregnancy was revealed, I let myself realize that I did not want another child. I remembered now, for the first time, that feeling of relief I used to have every time my monthly cycle reappeared. How had I let that slip from my awareness? I had never consciously changed my mind about wanting a child. It was my yogi's training, I suppose: to take what life offered and see it as a gift. I had been trying to smile at this gift. But at the same time, I must have been gritting my teeth, and I never even knew.

Michael had stayed in touch with this feeling throughout the pregnancy. This was how he could know his own relief the day the leaking had started to accelerate and I wore the blue shirt to the restaurant. But not I. I had buried that feeling the very instant I heard the news. Was this the final teaching? The final joke? It was almost laughable, in a horrible sort of way. What? This whole brouhaha, all these tears and suffering, over something I had never even wanted?

Oh, the irony of it all. All this sorrow. All the sympathy I had been getting. The deep looks, the offers of help, the mournful smiles and encouraging pats on the shoulder. A few chosen acquaintances knew the true story, knew that the pregnancy had been a wonder from beginning to end and that sympathy was not really needed. And perhaps, just perhaps, I could someday explain that to the others, to those who offered comfort. But this—how could I ever explain this? I could not.

I suddenly saw the Kashmir Shaivism of it all. Kashmir Shaivism: that little known philosophy of India, the doctrine that we are Shiva, we are the one who rouses himself from the emptiness, from the expanse of pure being, to create the universe. Like Shiva making the grand universe, so each of us makes our own little universe. Spiderlike, we secrete the silky threads of our own being, our own thoughts, to create the world we then inhabit. And sometimes, like Shiva, we are able to withdraw these silky threads back into ourselves, unraveling our little worlds.

I once had a vivid experience of this philosophy. It was on the day I was going home after a week at my meditation teacher's ashram. I had bought two oranges as parting gifts. One was for my work supervisor. But to whom should I give the other? I began to create a universe of possibilities. I had been in an exalted state, but now I began to descend from it, as thoughts started to crisscross mercilessly in my brain. Suddenly I had a moment of insight: If I, Shiva, was creating this whole universe, then I, Shiva, could withdraw it into myself. Literally. I sat cross-legged on my bed and watched in the mirror as I withdrew my universe of confusion by eating, calmly and deliberately, the second orange.

So now, I was seeing my universe dissolve. I had spun this pregnancy, spun this story, out of the silky threads of my own being. And now the pregnancy was withdrawn. And even the story was withdrawing, too. It was too much to hold. The thought was excruciating: This sorrow, this incredible, pure sorrow I had been feeling—all for something I had never even wanted. Oh, how the mind makes all.

Can you understand that, Lady? Can I? It was not that I did not want you. Never for an instant could that be true. I would never turn away from your light. But I could see now that although I wanted you, I did not want a child.

I tried to think whether there was anyone I knew who could understand this. I could share this with Michael, of course. But I was not sure there was any other person.

I walked softly back into the bedroom. I wanted to tell someone so that I could fix this in memory, lest I fall back asleep and lose this truth forever. And yet I did not want to wake Michael. As I slipped back in bed, I whispered his name—softly, so as not to wake him, but loud enough for me to remember. "Michael," I said softly, "what a blessing it is that we did not have a child."

Part Four

Something went out of my classroom that autumn. I could feel it going, and I remember the moment I knew that it was gone.

It was early in the morning the day of our last class before Christmas vacation. I had stayed up past midnight the night before to prepare Christmas gifts for my students, and had risen at 5:00 in the morning to finish them. I had bought an assortment of seashells and other beautiful natural objects for gifts. I was selecting an object to match the personality of each student and then writing a note making the connection. In addition, I needed to gather baking supplies because we would be baking bread that day in class. Sitting at the dining room table completing those notes, I felt exhausted.

I had to force myself to finish the notes. Up until then everything I did for my class was out of love. But this morning, for the first time, love was not guiding my hands. I kept going, though. I had to. Those gifts were an intention from the time of pregnancy, from the days when you were filling me with love. I could never go back on a promise made then. But I knew that there would not be such promises again. Never again would I spend myself so recklessly on my students. For when we lost circle and breath count—or was it when I lost the baby?—something went out of my class forever.

I am not surprised that the opposing parents, and some of the staff, I am sure, did not want our classroom to be the way it was—a kind of greenhouse, as I saw it, an experiment in love. They saw something threatening in our ways, something that went against the grain of what public school is for. But it puzzled me that Diane had been the one to pull the plug on our experiment. For she was someone who, like me, had the eye to see and value it.

My classroom remained a friendly place. And I know, having seen such friendly places when my children were in them, what a treasure they can be. But what we had before was something rarer, more exciting. And to this day I ask myself what kind of universe this is, that chooses friendship when it could have love.

I never was able to satisfy what I took to be the dual requirements of my job: the task of keeping twenty-five students quiet and busy, which is the main unstated mandate of any public school, and my own self-imposed mandate of keeping them alive and conscious. Perhaps the two are in conflict: after all, live people do not want to sit quietly all day. Or perhaps I simply did not have the skill to find a balance.

All I know is that despite the friendship I still felt for my students, teaching became more and more difficult. I began to dread the three days a week I had to face my second social studies class. Verbal requests had no effect on the superintendent, but after sending him a letter, I finally managed to get rid of my "class of sheep"—which shows the power of the written word. From then on I taught social studies to my own class only and had a mixed class for science, which turned out to be my favorite subject to teach. But no matter what small improvements were made, the task of teaching strained me to my limit.

At the end of any long vacation I would sink into despair. It was difficult to return after Christmas and almost impossible by the time my February break drew near its end. I was in a state of fierce anxiety. Also there was turmoil over the decision which I thought would soon be mine to make: whether to stay on another year or quit.

I expected my contract to be renewed in spring. After all, my classroom was a place where students flourished. And I was afraid that I would say yes to this job, which was clearly making me nervous and exhausted, out of fear of "the abyss," of the empty time at home which had gnawed at me in earlier years, bringing on depression. In addition, my mind offered two more, mutually opposed, reasons for me to stay with the job.

I was always trying to fathom the laws of the universe. One great principle, I thought, was to waste nothing. And since I was a good teacher, with the students of my class growing bigger inside, not just older and more tired of life, according to that principle I could not stop. On the other hand, there seemed to be a principle that a person should acquire all virtues and abilities to be complete. I obviously had not mastered teaching, had not learned to teach with ease and grace, without depleting the energy at my life's core. Therefore, by the second principle, I could not stop. In short, I was too good and not good enough to quit.

Confused and too tired from teaching to hear my own voices or even to read my heart, I overcame years of resistance and went to see Arlene, a local psychic known for having easy access to her guides. I bided my time as the psychic read some past lives by looking at my palm and then as soon as a pause permitted, told her of my anguish. I said my life was greatly diminished, hardly worth living as I now felt. She remarked that I was very sensitive and had been absorbing my students' problems, even the impressions of their home lives, which was part of what was draining me.

I asked her why I had wanted this job so desperately, why I needed to be teaching in the first place. She paused, closing her eyes to consult with her guidance. Then she gave me a look that was both sympathetic and amused, and said with a laugh, "I don't think you need to be." My reaction was amused outrage: "What! All this suffering, and it wasn't even in my cosmic script! Then what was it for?" Arlene paused to consult within again, gave another laugh, and answered, "I feel that what brought you there is to show you what you *don't* want."

I felt released. When I left, my anxiety had lifted. I no longer feared that I would blindly accept another year of teaching. I knew I would have the strength to say no or the courage to say yes. I could choose freely now and take my heart's desire. I expected to accept renewal when it came in the spring, and then review my decision after school ended, as soon as I had more perspective and my energy was restored. I must have known, though, that I would not be coming back. For from my first drive to school after that February break, I began severing my ties with the town of Southborough.

Driving through town every morning, I would wonder how that would feel when I was no longer on my way to work. The very houses, I knew, would look different to me. And the school building itself: In what file would it be stored in memory? The bitter title came to mind, "Jails I Once Served In." What a change these months had brought. It was only last summer that I had sighed on our way to Cape Cod over every elementary school we passed, and filed it under the title, "Heavens I Want To Enter."

On Thursday of my first week back in February, the principal came in with some "bad" news. There had been a school committee meeting to discuss renewals, the opposition had surfaced again and shown they were determined. A minimum number of days was required legally for notice of termination and, because the deadline was almost upon them, some townspeople had vowed to open Town Hall, just before midnight if necessary, to get those notices out in time to reserve their privilege of firing me. Diane thought the fight would be dirty—with Mrs. Braski dredging up any accusation she could think of. She recommended that I resign. And if I did so before the weekend, I could spare the other nontenured teachers the shock of receiving warnings of nonrenewal.

I felt little inside me except a vague sense of rightness and relief. And I could hear Mrs. Braski's words, "That's disgusting," echoing dimly in my mind. Five days after the birth, when I first returned to school, a student in my second social studies class asked me what was done with the baby. Innocent and open as always, I answered with the truth, which gave Mrs. Braski a fresh weapon for her arsenal. She came to a school committee meeting soon after that and, bypassing all rules of protocol, managed to publicly blast me, ending her speech with the complaint that I had had the nerve to tell my students that the baby was cremated. Her final outraged comment: "That's disgusting!"

The incident made little impression on me except for this last remark. I found it so unbelievable that I checked with several witnesses to verify. It did not surprise me that a person would be intolerant. But for an adult to be so shameless, so *publicly* intolerant: this I found astonishing. Disgusting? There is little that disgusts me. Cruelty, perhaps. But certainly not customs embedded in traditions not my own.

It was Mrs. Braski's remark, I suppose, that led me to resign so quickly. I realized that there was no limit to the charges she might make against me. And I knew that this was an opponent I did not care to fight. Without reflection and without consulting anyone—naively, I suppose—I handed in my resignation that very day.

The remark "That's disgusting!" was quite in vogue at school, and as time went on I grew allergic to it. Where I had once dismissed it as silly and harmless, now I saw in each child who said it a budding Mrs. Braski and vowed I would not let it go unchallenged.

I remember watching a video on tigers with my science class. A tigress had stalked her prey majestically, then pounced on it and killed it, and was dragging the carcass back to her lair. "That's disgusting!" called out a student. "Is it?" I asked. We were in the cafeteria, and I scanned rapidly, casting about for an idea. "I wonder what a tiger would find disgusting in our human ways. Maybe eating with a fork and knife?" I knew how terribly lame my response was. But I had made myself a promise which I had to keep.

My students arranged a lovely surprise party for me when they learned I would not be coming back. They kept it from me for weeks, though it took tremendous planning. There were decorations, refreshments, a bouquet from them to me, some gifts, and a booklet of signatures and testimonials, with my favorite comment, "Strange but fun." They had even put together a poetry reading in deference to my taste, following a hint from Diane. And there was a gigantic paper-rocket contest, with individually designed rockets and a multitude of criteria: longest flight, most surprising flight, silliest flight, and so on.

It was the usual wild, chaotic affair. It was beautiful. And they had done it all. They brought back a touch of your golden love that day.

As the love in my class waned, my love for Michael grew stronger. The hour we would spend together in bed before the day was started was for me a magic hour, by far the most real portion of each day. There were no words worth noting, no extraordinary embraces. As individuals we did nothing memorable. But I clung to Michael in my need, and it seemed to me we fused. Had our corporate presence been able to speak, it would have said: "We are one. For this brief time our truest, twinned nature comes to life, only to subside again when, as two, we leave this room." For me this hour was a zone of enchantment, the island where the divine lovers Krishna and Radha dwelt. Though wars might rage outside, with us there was only closeness and peace.

I had once read a book which presents the view that we humans are kept by Someone as cows are kept by humans—for our milk. The "milk" that Someone wants, and uses for his own purposes, is our emotions—the purer and the more intense, the better. Anger, jealousy—any emotion will do. But the prime emotion is love, which is given the name "loosh." I can remember getting out of bed one morning and realizing that this was loosh. Suddenly I understood the author's point of view. If I were Someone, I, too, would want to harvest this. It was the highest-octane fuel, the most powerful human love, that I had ever known.

This magic lasted until the end of spring, when I was finally certain I would survive the school year. And then our morning hour went back to normal. Perhaps our fusion needed my fear and desperation to fuel it. Or perhaps this was your final departure from me. I know only that we were both disappointed at the loss.

In February I had asked Arlene what she could see about the pregnancy, saying that for me it had been, from beginning to end, the darshan of a saint. She confirmed my view, saying that she saw a circle of angelic beings above me and that the being of the pregnancy was one of those. "I see a beautiful, beautiful spirit," she told me. "A woman. Just radiant. Full of light. Full of expansion, love—unconditional love. I think your description of a saint is accurate." It was her closing words which moved me most: "She came not to be born but to touch you—because she loves you."

Hearing that, I felt the grace of it all. Not just that you had come to visit me, which may be a common grace. (After all, how many pregnancies, how many life events contain a visitation from beyond?) But I was awed at the further grace, to me extraordinary, that I had been given the eye to see the visit, the heart to feel your presence.

Two months later some new information came to me, a matching piece to what I already knew about you, which gave a new dimension to our relationship. In April, in connection with Michael's large lecture course, we had as guests at our house Pat Rodegast, famous for channeling a guide named Emmanuel, and her co-worker, Judith Stanton. I was still suffering greatly from the teaching and wondering what would become of me next year, now that I had lost my job. Naturally I secretly hoped for a consultation with Emmanuel. But when I met Pat and Judith, and realized how besieged Pat must be with such requests, I resolved to ask for nothing.

We had dinner shortly after their arrival, and Michael asked Judith, in casual conversation, what sort of work she did. Judith answered that she worked with healing. "There's someone here who can use some healing," said Michael, and looked at me. At this, my hostess' decorum forgotten, I burst into tears. They were sympathetic, Pat immediately suggesting a talk with Emmanuel after dinner and Judith giving me some vigorous back-rubbing during the meal. When dinner was over, Pat set a candle on the table, took a moment, and then Emmanuel was there.

I have heard many a channeled voice and not been impressed. But this was a darshan of the heart, like the one with Genesis. Once again I felt touched from the inside. Emmanuel spoke long and lovingly to me of loving myself, of rescuing the lost and frightened child inside me, which alone could cure my suffering and show me my next step. His words were helpful, and also the atmosphere he created. For in it I could sense the possibility of my own self-love. But what was most potent for my knowing you was a remark which Pat made just as she was coming back to everyday consciousness.

It was her last remark before the candle was blown out, and I could not tell whether she made it as Emmanuel or as herself. She said, "I'm not hearing more . . ." meaning, I suppose, that Emmanuel's voice was gone. And then she added, "I'm seeing a spirit with you now—light—beautiful—feels feminine. Someone you've known is there—even though you ought not to have." A mild laugh. A sigh. And Pat was back.

"Someone you've known is there—even though you ought not to have." When she said those words, dear one, I knew that she meant you.

The morning after Pat and Judith's visit, as I was driving to school, I suddenly had the thought, "Me and my Golden Lady are driving in." Where did this thought come from? It took me by surprise. Its very lack of grammar was revealing; for correct grammar has always come naturally to me.

It was this thought, dear one, that gave me a sense of partnership with you. Arlene had implied you were an angel, one of a host. But now, for the first time, I felt you as an individual, as a partner and a friend. I felt I knew you, and I even knew your name. For the first time it became possible that I would some day tell your story.

School was sweet that day. I had gone to a workshop given by Pat and Judith the day before, and I wrote in big letters on the blackboard one of Emmanuel's aphorisms from the workshop: "Truth without love is fact." We discussed this a bit in class: What are facts good for, and is their value limited? And I asked myself some private questions: Is not school the very worshipping place of facts, the temple of "truth without love"? And can love be part of school?

That day my teaching was inspired. I thought of new approaches to books in reading group that clarified the theme of love. And in science I came up with all sorts of dynamic inquiries to bring home hard concepts for the students. I forgot myself completely in the intensity of teaching, and so I forgot about you.

But toward the end of the day, when I passed the mirror in the bathroom, I saw my reflection and remembered.

I looked at myself, but it was you whom I addressed: "We've had a nice day, haven't we?"

And what had we been doing, my partner and I? I stared into the mirror and the answer came: "Giving out golden light."

It was your light, I knew. I could picture the gold vividly, like the piece of cheap, glittery golden net in my attic.

I kept looking into my eyes, waiting for a final comment, and it came: "Well, that's what the light is for, isn't it?"

This seemed as good a summary of life as I would ever have. What else is there to do but give out golden light?

Although the loss of my job was a relief, I was also bitter over the way it had been lost. All that spring, driving to school, I would speak out loud to the town in an attempt to reach some closure and to ease my pain.

Each morning on my way to Southborough, I would pass the elementary school of Allwood, known for its excellence. Both towns shared an unusual tax bounty; the difference was that the people in Allwood had voted to spend a large portion of the town's tax revenue on their school, while the people in Southborough voted every year to lower taxes rather than improve the school. Thinking of the dismal lack of free time for teachers, the dearth of good textbooks, and the noisy, overcrowded cafeteria, I would begin my oration: "Oh, cheapskate Southborough—"

Then I would feel a pang of remorse as I remembered the many wonderful parents who had helped with class—Brad's mother, who came in after night shift to help us make our pizza lunch, Laney Barnes and her husband, who had done such wonderful social studies presentations, or Serena's mother, who taught my students patchwork quilting, bringing in fabric and even ironing for them—and I would correct my salutation: "Oh, cheapskate-generous, horrible-wonderful Southborough—"

Passing some houses in the town, I would continue speaking, usually to the opposition. "Don't be afraid for your children. I won't change them. It would be lucky if I could. But our time together is too short. Do not worry. They will come back just as you want them, just as you sent them."

I would ponder what had brought together this unlikely combination, the parents of Southborough and myself. With some I was rightly linked, through mutual appreciation. But with the opposition? "They say that whenever we meet someone, there is a reason, we have done something to deserve it. I don't know what I've done to deserve you. (I don't remember committing any crimes.) And I'm sure you're wondering what you've done to deserve me."

Arriving at school, I would close my oration, always on the same reassuring note. "Well, our time together is coming to an end. Do not worry. Soon it will be over."

One morning in June as I drove to school, I finally did arrive at a reason for the combination, and came closer to a sense of reconciliation with the town. I often used to ponder what my year would have been had I taken the other teaching job, at the private school, where parents would have been appreciative of my approach. I had chosen the Southborough job for the sake of opportunity and challenge. But driving in that morning, I saw that there was something more important, a cosmic reason why I had to choose that job: I needed it for you to visit me. I needed all the strain and suffering to call you to me, to draw your grace. And perhaps I needed the suffering to soften me as well, so I would be receptive to your visit.

I know this seems impossible. After all, I was already pregnant when I took the job. (Or was I? There was no firm evidence until October.) But as many times as I pondered this, I always reached the same conclusion: If the universe had known that I was not going to accept the Southborough job, I would not have become pregnant. Or, if I had, it would not have been with you.

I truly believe that somewhere in my choice of Southborough was your choice of me. And so I realize that if I could transcend my human limitations, I would be grateful to Mrs. Braski as to my greatest friend. And I would thank the town of Southborough for taking me in so that I could welcome you.

I often pondered the mystery of how Mrs. Braski had managed, almost single-handedly, to deprive the town's children of my teaching. It was the parent of a first-grader who gave me my answer. Seeing me on the playground one day in June, he approached and introduced himself. "You know," he said, "I'm sorry for the town, almost ashamed for us. Somehow, without our even knowing it, we let ourselves be represented by Mrs. Braski. It wasn't just ignorance. I think it was fear, too. When someone is that irrational, one shies away. There is a great reluctance to enter into the fray with someone of her caliber."

I understood him perfectly. By creating an atmosphere of fear and distaste around her, Mrs. Braski easily managed to get her way. Had it not been fear that had led me to resign so quickly?

There were people in town who supported me, and many more who would have supported me had they only known. But who had motivation to match Mrs. Braski's—to make the issue known and rally people to my cause? This was the crux of the matter for me: My supporters were always *individuals*, while my opponents formed a group. There was something disturbing in this for me. Was I being shown a darker cosmic law: the greater power of the *negative* to coalesce?

The whole episode still raises disturbing questions for me. I had always wondered about the people of Nazi Germany. I knew there must have been many fine people who for some reason had not spoken out. Now the silent people of Southborough were giving me a glimpse of how such things happen. And I, in my silence, was no different. There was ignorance and reluctance, yes. And there was—for me, at least—laziness and cowardice. I knew it would have been healthy for the town if I had stayed and fought. It would have forced the townspeople to examine their values, if not to change them. But that would have taken a generosity of spirit, which was not mine: I had no heart for the struggle.

I last saw Mrs. Braski at a school picnic our final week in June. The cooks had prepared bag lunches for the students, and my class was sitting, along with all the others, on the front lawn of the school.

We had nearly finished eating when one of the boys asked if he could pop his milk carton. I did my usual quick calculation: Anything that was remotely wild would make it harder for me to quiet my students in the clasroom. But on the other hand, popping a milk carton was so harmless. And it was a gesture of freedom, one of the few small freedoms they might have at school. Yes, I could afford my small loss for their gain. I was willing to make the sacrifice out of my care for them.

There was a series of small explosions on this beautiful summer day, as about twelve boys joyfully stamped on their milk cartons. With each pop I could feel an answering explosion of joy blossom in my heart, a small but triumphant Fourth of July.

I saw several teachers turning their heads my way. Then I noticed Mrs. Braski, who had come to give a message to her daughter's teacher. She was not looking at me, but I knew she was well aware of me, for she kept her face deliberately turned away. As the series of pops continued, she shot one quick glance my way and stalked off.

I had read the phrase "high dudgeon," but this was the first time I had seen it in operation! I could feel what Mrs. Braski was thinking as she walked off: "Hmph! I was right. This woman cannot even teach her students to behave."

I stared after her as she walked away, this enemy I was trying to see as my greatest friend. And then I turned my attention back to my students and heard the last echoes of the benediction which had been sounding in my heart: "Let a thousand milk cartons pop. May you enjoy these moments. May you be free."

Finally the impossible happened: It was the last day of school.

I had created some activities for closure, one a "Name That Tune" program, in which I sang or played music from our school year. When I hummed the song of the states, the students asked if they could sing it, to my surprise. This difficult song, with the fifty states in alphabetical order, had caused some grumbling when they had been asked to learn it. But in the end they were proud of their accomplishment.

For me this song will always have a touch of your gold. For when Eddy finally sang it without mistakes—the only hard task his depression allowed him to complete all year—the whole class burst into applause. And now they were asking to sing it one last time.

Usually my students would not sing with their full voices, and I often urged them to let go more and raise their voices louder. On this last day of school, they almost lifted the roof off with their singing. Each child sang, practically shouted, at fullest volume, and there was no one in the building who did not hear our song.

There was something special in that singing, some message to be deciphered. Were my students showing me that they could sing loudly after all? Was it a final good-bye? Was it a release of all the pent-up energy of the year—from all the hours of sitting at their desks when they wanted to roam, standing in line when they wanted to cluster, staying quiet when they wanted to make noise? We had studied the Declaration of Independence. And now, with the energy of that song, my students were declaring themselves free.

A small miracle occurred that day. Our room was due to be painted early the next morning, and all chairs and desks had to be removed. This meant we had to sit on the floor. And so we got to have one final circle. I asked my students what they would remember years from now about this class, and we went around the circle.

Many of the students talked about how terrible it had been with the substitute teachers when I took my week off for the pregnancy.

Other students spoke about how strange they thought I was in the beginning. "But now you don't seem strange at all," said Mary Ann, while others nodded in agreement. (Ah, so they had learned my language.) And Stuart added, with a peculiar grin, that class had been "weird, strange, and boring."

So many memories crowded that the students asked to go around the circle again, each one with a different memory—except Stuart, who repeated with same fixed grin, "Weird, strange, and boring." I felt for him. He was the only student in my class with a large measure of "sheep." Rigid in his expectations and frustrated all year by my teaching style, he had always been a perfect gentleman about it and was still trying to be. All I could do was appreciate him. I hoped that some of the freedom of our classroom would remain stored in his soul, to be drawn upon some day when he was ready.

When Mary Ann's second turn came, she repeated how weird they had found me in the beginning. "But after you lost your baby and then some people in town started giving you a hard time, we really pulled together." She was the one who had organized the party for me, for which the class had shown appreciation by voting her a citizenship award that month, in one of our rare landslide victories. So: for all my attempts to foster a sense of unity, it had been the miscarriage which worked the best.

During the first round Jonathan had shared his shock and horror when, fishing rod in hand on a day of playing hooky, he had gotten a telephone call from me telling him to get to school at once for a dress rehearsal! Now he closed our second round, and his brief comment, I suspect, summed up the year for many: "When I remember this year, I will remember you." How not? I had shared myself so fully with these students, more than with any other group.

And now, I suppose, another small miracle occurred. I began to learn discretion. I had toyed all year with the idea of telling my class on the last day about my little game of omitting "to the flag" in our morning pledge of allegiance, for I was curious whether any of them had noticed. But when the time came, I thought, "What would be the point?" I had done it as an attempt at honesty, but if my students could not understand, they might feel tricked and lose their trust. And so I did not tell.

The greatest exercise in discretion came during the final moments of school, when I turned down one last opportunity to be weird. It was in connection with the spider web in the ring of gold which had hung all year from the ceiling of our classroom.

It seemed appropriate to me that my last act of the year would be to undo my first. And so I had planned to cut the web down as my final act. I had also planned to sing a loud and heartfelt *Shehechiyanu*, a Hebrew blessing said at the beginning of holidays which thanks God for having survived until this day. (How often I had doubted that I would!) And I thought I would explain that blessing to my class.

But somehow, as I looked at all those dear faces, I could not do it. At that last moment I felt that my quota of weirdness had finally been used up. They had been so beautiful, so accommodating all year, had stretched themselves toward me in so many ways. I could not ask them to stretch one more time.

And so I stood on a chair, scissors in hand, and I hummed a soft *Shehechiyanu* to myself, my final benediction for this precious group about to be dispersed forever.

Looking down at my students, I felt what the year had been. It had been full of suffering and exhaustion, yes. But also it had been full of visitation and grace.

Long afterwards, I would look back and see that this was

~ℑ~

one of the most terrible years of my life. But also one of the best: because it was so full of love, and so fully lived.

I cut down the spider web in a ring of gold. There were report cards to be handed out. And then, a realization that left one breathless: The buses were here! It was over.

Epilogue

The tale is ended, dear one. I have written you a love letter; I will not deny it.

I once heard that woodpeckers peck not only to find food but also to find a mate. They tap out their message, waiting for a response. In spring I listen to the medley of bird voices, and the tapping too, and marvel. Everyone is searching for a mate, each announcing in its own notes: "I am here. Are you there? I am here. Are you there?" Over and over the message is called in blue-jay language, in nuthatch language, in woodpecker language, and in all of nature's other tongues.

❧

So now I sit, woodpecker-like, and tap out my message to you on the typewriter keys. "I am here, Lady. Are you there?" I am hoping for a response. I want to meet you once again, face to face, as I did on the day of the birth.

When I lost the baby, some friendly Southborough teachers offered me their sympathy. I always felt uncomfortable returning their sympathetic looks with the expected look of sorrow and of being comforted. But what else could I do? It was too difficult to tell them how wonderful the birth had been—too strange and long a story.

Once school was over, I found myself reliving those moments of sympathy with growing unease, as if I were being caught in a lie. I thought that if I wrote your story, I might make up for my lapse in openness. And I was challenged, too. Could I tell the story of your visit in such a way that others could understand what the pregnancy had meant for me?

I slipped into writing as comfortably as a person settles into sleep. To sit and type your story was as natural as breathing, and I would come away refreshed, as if from meditation or deep sleep. Writing, I was at home with the universe and with myself. And that is how I learned I was a writer.

And so this is another of your gifts to me. I know your bounty and am not surprised. You have ended by giving me the gift of my own self.

I know that some will question this story, saying it is the product of imagination, of an overfertile mind. And even I am willing to entertain this thought. But I have decided to maintain this story, at least for now. For I know something of how life works.

I am embarrassed at having reached the age of forty-three with so few truths to show for it. But two truths I have lived and these I truly own: The first is that we have nothing to share with others except ourselves. The second is that our stories live only by our commitment to them and that our lives are what we declare them to be.

I understand that human bravery is just this: to live in the awareness that there is no truth except the truth we make. It is not easy to endure this paradox, that truth is what we make, that it is *we* who choose whatever truths we wish to live by and maintain.

Most people manage to avoid this awareness, not realizing that this, too, is a choice. Some pay no attention to beliefs, immersing themselves in the diversions of pleasure and pain, which the world offers in abundance. Others take refuge in the "rightness" of their views, claiming to believe them because they are true—in the name of which much violence has been done.

To live with this awareness is the path of few. Sometimes I find it lonely—and frightening, too. But there is also an excitement. For life with this awareness takes on the qualities of a continual free fall.

I see that the choice is ours. As long as we acknowledge this choice and live with it—face the absurdity, which is also the freedom—shall we not be both tolerant and brave?

Your ashes, by the way, are with me still. The ground was cold and unwelcoming in November, and then was frozen over winter. We expected to scatter your ashes on our land in spring, after the ground thawed. But when spring came, I could not bring myself to part with them. They had become my talisman, my sign. I chose to make them my proof of the unprovable: that the divine really *does* visit the human, even troubling to take on a human form.

I often pass your ashes on my way to write your story. Sometimes I salute them with a slight nod of the head. And other times I stop to sit. I sit very quietly. And I feel the words of your story rise around me like the droplets of a mist.